Rev. Ramon M. Frank

Extraordinary Living for Ordinary Men

I am again struck by the freshness, the directness, and the aptness of what Sam Shoemaker preached and wrote. Sam's theology was not of the mothball but of the fireball variety. Never content to write about *faith, he wrote* from *faith and he wrote* of *faith.*

DR. PAUL S. REES

Extraordinary Living for Ordinary Men

Excerpts selected from the writings of Sam Shoemaker by his daughter, Helen Shoemaker Rea, and the Staff of Faith at Work

ZONDERVAN PUBLISHING HOUSE
GRAND RAPIDS   MICHIGAN

Extraordinary Living for Ordinary Men

Copyright 1965 by
Zondervan Publishing House
Grand Rapids, Michigan

First printing.....September, 1965
Second printing...September, 1965
Third printing ....December, 1965
Fourth printing.......April, 1966
Fifth printing..........July, 1966
Sixth printing.....November, 1966
Seventh printing.......April, 1967

Library of Congress Catalog Card Number 65-19501

Printed in the United States of America

Contents

Introduction

By any measure you care to use, Sam Shoemaker was one of the most remarkable Christians of our time. As a Canon in the Episcopal Church, he was a prominent churchman, successful both as the rector of two large parishes and as a leader in the affairs of his denomination. He was one of the great preachers of America, consistently filling two "downtown" churches with people from near and far, as well as being one of the most sought-after guest speakers in the country. He was the author of dozens of books, which have had a profound effect on both the church and the world, since they were read by seekers and church leaders alike.

But Dr. Sam will probably best be remembered as an evangelist by the thousands all over the world who remember first meeting the living Christ and feeling His touch in one of Dr. Sam's sermons or during one of his innumerable unhurried conversations with individuals. Counseling, or life-changing conversations with individuals from all walks of life, was what he loved most of all.

As I have tried to understand the spiritual greatness and tremendous effectiveness that underlay all of Sam's ministry, marking it as clearly apostolic, three things stand out. First, he was captured by the power and the love of a living Christ, convinced that He truly was the Lord of all and able to transform *any* person, relationship, situation, or organization wholly given to Him.

His second characteristic was a belief in the "now-ness" of the Gospel. He knew that the Christian faith had the only relevant word for man's past or future, but he believed that the present was the Holy Spirit's primary concern for men and nations. His challenge always was, "If you believe in Jesus Christ, what are you doing about it now?"

Finally, in seeing life through the eyes of his Master, he recaptured the basic strategy of the New Testament, in that he was always impressed by the possibilities of the ordinary. He saw in ordinary men and circumstances the means and the weapons by which God could change the world. One example is A.A. (Alcoholics Anonymous), which calls Sam Shoemaker its spiritual founder. He believed that two drunks who found sobriety through the power of surrender to a living Christ could start a fellowship that could help other drunks. They did, and today tens of thousands of people owe their very lives to that conviction.

This book will help us all to see life and Christ as Sam Shoemaker did. May his kind increase!

BRUCE LARSON

Acknowledgment

Deep appreciation is expressed to the editors and staff of *Faith at Work* Magazine for their work in selecting and compiling the articles in this book — and for permission to reprint them in this fashion.

Extraordinary Living for Ordinary Men

1.

The Romance
of Real Religion

Going Far Enough for the Fun

W E SHALL THINK TOGETHER of the romance of real religion. And we shall have in the background of our thinking the story of Jesus and the Rich Young Ruler, together with the conversation which Jesus had with His disciples after the young man had gone away.

The story begins with this wealthy youth flinging himself impetuously before Jesus, and asking, "What shall I do that I may inherit eternal life?" Nothing is said about what brought him to Jesus in this way. The inference is that he saw something in Jesus which enormously attracted him. He may, in this phrase "eternal life," have been attempting to describe the quality he saw in Jesus which so much fascinated him, and which he wanted for himself.

Jesus begins with the Commandments, as if to say, "Remember that eternal life has a moral backbone. Do you keep the Commandments?" And with the naive complacency, the innocent conceit of the immature, the young man replied, "All these have I observed from my youth."

This sort of superb assurance, so often masking a pathetic inner insecurity, makes youth as lovable as it is exasperating; and Jesus did not reprimand him. "Jesus, beholding him, loved him."

Then He put His finger on the weak spot in this boy — his money: "One thing thou lackest: go thy way, sell whatsoever thou hast, and give to the poor, and thou shalt have treasure in heaven; and come, take up the cross, and follow me."

I do not believe that this was a universal command, but rather that it touched for this particular man the greatest rival to God as his ultimate security, namely his financial security. And the boy "was sad at that saying, and went away grieved; for he had great possessions."

Now the by-play and the commentary on that incident have always seemed to me almost more interesting and significant than the incident itself. The refusal of this young man to accept the challenge of Christ moves the Lord to say, "How hardly shall they that have riches enter into the Kingdom of God!" He says it is as hard as for a camel to go through a needle's eye. And the disciples ask, "Who then can be saved?"

Nowhere has the sheerness of Jesus' claims so struck them in all its fullness as now. Jesus had asked everything of the young man, and promised him nothing but treasure in heaven and a cross here. He had come with such enthusiasm, and gone away so crestfallen! But he had asked for something as if he wanted it. And Jesus had simply told him the truth, that the price of what he wanted was the kind of faith in God through acceptance of Christ which trusted no secondary security whatever.

This talk about costs and rewards, about crosses and joy long-deferred, began to stir thoughts in the minds of the disciples. Simon Peter, as so often was the case, voiced what they were all thinking, "Lo, we have left all and followed Thee," not implying, as I believe, self-praise, so much as wonderment about whether faith and the life of religion were worth what they cost. They were taking one last look at the blackened beams of burned bridges. They could not follow the young man who took his free way across the fields and was gone. They were committed. They were stuck. Was it really worth it?

Then Jesus did one of the most merciful and beautiful things He ever did. He did not chide Peter for his want of enthusiasm. Instead, He lifted him up, and in one heaped-up promise He showed him the romance of real religion, saying, "There is no man that hath left house, or brethren, or sisters, or mother, or father, or children, or lands for my sake, and for the Gospel's sake, but he shall receive a hundredfold now in this time, houses, and brethren, and sisters, and mothers, and children, and lands, with persecutions; and in the world to come eternal life."

Was ever man's self-interest rewarded by so fine a prospect held out before the eye of his imagination? Was ever prudential selfishness so gently dealt with, so effectually supplanted by a vision calculated to make it seem not so much sinful as unnecessary? Was ever the natural human desire for interest, happiness, and adventure in living ever more wonderfully laid hold upon in the interest of faith; or faith and the life of the Spirit shown more compellingly to be the fulfillment of that deep desire?

The question about whether the game is worth the candle in religion is as new today as it was then. We know that when religion gets going in any life, it tends to be increasingly absorbing, and may ask for the denial, not only of great and wicked things, but also of some small and in themselves harmless things if they, by emphasis or tendency, hinder in the primary business of following Christ. Jesus still asks everything. He does not always ask us to stop doing all the things we used to do, or that the world is doing round about us, but He does ask that we submit to Him the question whether we shall do them or not. He will arbitrate, and sometimes, of course, He will forbid.

No man can have attempted to take Jesus seriously, to swing into spiritual stride with the elemental and obvious demands of Christianity, leaving behind him the things which have cluttered and preoccupied his time and stolen his attention from God, without feeling some fine day a misgiving sweep across his mind that maybe, after all, the whole life of faith and religion is not worth while, and costs more than it comes to. Jesus' answer to this is that the thing men all want is happiness, the happiness of a life with drive and purpose in it, and that, to this need, the answer which He brings is the romance of real religion.

Now, I want you to remember that when Jesus held out this great reward of the romance of true religion, He was talking not to the world in general, but to a group of committed men. The Rich Young Ruler was gone. So were the Pharisees who appeared earlier in the story. He spoke to men who had cast their die—His own disciples. They were not curiosity-seekers, nor safe and sane traditionalists

—no selfish, money-grubbing fellows who served their own interests all week and then dressed up in fine clothes on Sunday and walked down the avenue to church. They were men with their coats off. They were in this thing with Him to the death.

Some of them had given up their ordinary livelihood and work, and were trusting God for daily bread as well as for daily inspiration. The men to whom He held out the romance of religion were men who had paid the price of religion. And the price of romance in religion is the price of romance everywhere else—single-mindedness. You can't pursue a dozen ways of life at once; nor serve a dozen spiritual masters. There is fun in religion—heaps of it, quantities of it—for those who go far enough for fun.

LET us see wherein the romance of real religion consists:

First of all, there is the most colossal romance in cooperating with the Spirit that controls this universe. For the Christian, the universe is instinct with purpose. He cannot conceive of this unimaginably vast cosmos without conscious intelligence behind it, nor of that gigantic intelligence creating without purpose. If there be a will for the whole, there must be a will for the part. The oak tree and the stars play their parts compelled. You and I play ours invited. God gives us the option: we can cooperate if we will or we can refuse.

Most normal human beings enjoy being part of a great project. That joy is not confined to those who conceive it —it extends on out to the last workman who brings it to completion, provided he shares in the great conception. The

The Romance of Real Religion [17]

riveter who sealed the final bolt on the bridge and the painter who painted the last girder were as needful as the engineer. No job is little which is part of the whole. The romance comes from sharing the great conception, and knowing our part to play, and playing it in such a way that the whole is brought to perfection.

You and I may be only very simple workmen in that vast bridge God is trying to fling across the river which divides the world of the Spirit from the world of sense, but we can help if we will with the completion of that enormous enterprise. How one longs to see some of the people who are grubbing along, reduced to their own powers, their own little patches, their own little private purposes, lifted up into cooperation with the majestic plans of Almighty God! And if you believe there is no romance in that, I'll dare you to make the experiment and try!

NEXT there is the romance of relationship. There is the great relationship between God and those who honestly love and seek His will. There is a Person at the heart of things. We can talk with Him and cooperate and plan and rejoice and be serious, just as we can with the person closest in all the world to us. God is not that kind of person to many, and for good reason—they have wanted other things more than Him, or refused to surrender something He wants them to surrender, or never taken time enough to be really with Him in prayer. Vaguely some of us believe in Him, but we have not found Him. But you can find Him. He is there to be found. And when you find Him, you will find joy with Him, such joy as you never knew without Him.

But there is also the kind of relationship which comes to

pass between those who find themselves thus cooperating with God. I think that I know something of the joy of ordinary friendship where the relation arises out of common interests, between those whose personalities strike the mysterious spark called congeniality. But that is very meagre beside the relationships of those whose lives are integrated into the same great plan of God, and who work together with complete honesty and accord, dealing in the truth with love, sharing in the perfectly glorious work of making God and His Holy Spirit a reality to other people through Jesus Christ.

Then there is the romance of a fight. When I mentioned cooperation with God's will awhile ago, some of you may have been saying, "Yes, but I am a rebel. I would rather dissent than agree." Now, I am pointing out to you about where your dissent ought to come in. You and I have in our veins the blood of men who fought, who had to fight, and loved to fight. They fought for their food, they fought for their wives, and they fought for their existence. Even if we some day succeed in banishing war from the world, what are we going to do with all this fighting essence in us which we call red blood? Well, if we are wise we are going to remember that there are still plenty of enemies to conquer, enemies of mankind—ignorance, sickness, greed, sin. There is an age-long war on, between good and evil, between God and hell, between the forces that make for life and the forces that make for death.

Christianity believes that there is one place of strategic importance in that warfare, and that is the set of the individual human soul. It believes you have to begin there. The right set of the human soul is the set Godward. When that set is right, the manward set is right also. When you are committed to God's great plan manifested in Christ, you are part of a continuous warfare to free the souls of men from ignorance, selfishness, and sin.

If you think this is a tame little tea party, again I dare you to come into it. You will find plenty of very real enemies, who put up a very real fight. But you will also know the kind of spiritual joy which made George Whitefield, that warrior of the Spirit of the eighteenth century, say, "There is not much romance of a fight in sitting in a pew and paying the missionaries to go where the battle is hot; but there is quite a good deal of the romance of a fight in any life that dares today to take an uncompromising stand for Jesus Christ, and begins to campaign on enemy territory and win the pagans away to the new life which is in Him."

AND then there is the romance of a risk. Every gentleman is some kind of gambler. Every decent man throws his life away on something better than himself—a career, a woman he loves, or a great cause. The Anglo-Saxon is as full of the love of a sporting chance as he is of red blood. Do you think Christ wants to cool all that out of him? Not a bit of it. He wants to capture that for His Kingdom. To what did He appeal when He stopped beside a lake and called to a batch of fishermen, "Come ye after me, and I will make you to become fishers of men," if not to their love for bigger game than fish out of a lake?

Religion is a risk. You can't indisputably prove or disprove the very existence of God on which religion is founded. Donald Hankey says that religion is betting your life there is a God. The odds seem to some of us overwhelmingly on the side of faith. But not in this world shall we finally know. The romance of religion is the romance of a risk. Some of us have flung everything we have got into it. There are only two alternatives here—God is, or He isn't. You leap one way or the other. It is a risk to take, to bet everything you have on God. So is it a risk not to.

So many stand just outside the greatest joy that can come to any human being this side of the grave—the joy of conscious fellowship with God and with those to whom He is the one great living reality. Some of us are unhappy, and some have accepted unhappiness as a fate, when actually it is a problem. You are poor when you might be rich. You have nothing when you might possess all things. You are going through life like a drudge when you ought to go through it like a crusader. You are half-way committed to Christ, and you have your reward in a heart which is half-happy.

Do you want the romance of real religion? Then pay the price of real religion. Let your life go into the hands of God. Do you want to go on with the mediocre, uninspired, tepid existence . . . or with the indulgent and sinful and wasteful existence . . . which has been yours in the past? There is a so much better way.

2.

How to Find Faith

Steps for the Honest Doubter

MOST PEOPLE IN the world envy a person who has a strong religious faith. They may hold that such a person has not sufficiently used his brains, nor considered the objections that the prevailing secularism can oppose to religious belief. But I think even the most skeptical or materialistic knows that a real believer is a happier and richer person than he, and envies him his faith, even while saying that it is impossible for him.

We can no longer say that ours is a particularly unbelieving age, although we can and must say that the prevalent philosophy in many places is naturalism or humanism. Within this society there are many who have become conditioned to unbelief, and grow up disposed toward it. Some are that way by nature.

Such a person was Jesus' disciple Thomas, one of the Twelve. He was not only an intellectual skeptic; he was a temperamental skeptic. He always looked on the dark side of things—witness most of what is said about him in the

New Testament. And confronted with the possibility that Jesus had risen from the dead, he said flatly, "Except I shall see in his hands the print of the nails, and put my finger into the print of the nails . . . I will not believe." He was not going to be pushed into anything by someone's emotion. He was steeled against it.

Thomas is a good person for the skeptic of our time to follow. He was determined not to believe without evidence. But he made his condition, and if the condition was met, that opened up a new possibility. Eight days after Easter night, when Thomas made his declaration of unbelief, Jesus met him. He said to Thomas, "Reach hither thy finger, and see my hands; and reach hither thy hand, and put it into my side: and be not faithless, but believing."

On evidence, Thomas was convinced. And he said, "My Lord and my God." Jesus then spoke to him and spoke to us all at the same time, "Because thou hast seen me, thou hast believed. Blessed are they that have not seen, and yet have believed." That was the night when Thomas reversed himself. That was the night when a declaration of unbelief was changed into a declaration of belief.

He had received the kind of evidence that we all must have if we are truly to believe. You see, faith is not so much like coming to accept a philosophy; it is much more like falling in love. The total personality is involved—something more than reason—a kind of overwhelming response with many factors called into play.

We sometimes forget that unbelief also can be emotional. A very pagan young woman said to me defiantly one day, "I don't believe in God." And I said to her, "This might be due to two things: (1) your despair about your own incorrigibility, which you rationalize into a theory that there is

How to Find Faith [23]

no hope, and therefore no God; or (2) your knowing that, if there is a God, He wants you to live very differently from the way you are living now." I remember her saying, "You might have something there." Starting from that place, she began facing herself honestly, and she wound up with a very strong faith in Christ.

There are many people in the world who have no idea how to break that kind of a deadlock in themselves. When they try to break out of it, they can't do it. This failure constitutes about nine-tenths of their unbelief.

Have you read that remarkable book called *The Tragic Sense of Life* (which is anything but tragic) by Unamuno? There is a poignant sentence in it which goes, "Those who deny God deny Him because of their despair at not finding Him." I am convinced that is profoundly true, psychologically and spiritually. Now what are the ways by which people can reasonably and experimentally break out of the circle of skepticism and unbelief?

The first step is admit that you would like to believe. You can look in any direction you like, and you will see people in whose lives faith is providing adventure, purpose, courage, integration, or an increase of sheer vitality. You will also, if you look closely enough, see people in whose lives unbelief produces aimlessness, drift, fear, dissipation of energy, and a contraction of natural powers.

I know there are hundreds who forsake faith, and seem to do all right—for a time. A man will not starve because he misses a few meals. People live on what they had. They live on what other people have, and what society has. This parasitic existence can go on a long time. But how often does restlessness, or lassitude, or nervousness, or a breakdown lie at the end of the trail?

Face these things. Admit to yourself that faith is better than no faith. We who believe may not always be as good people as some conscientious people who disbelieve, but we are in touch with more Power. Admit the incompleteness of life without faith, without God. Admit the increased meaningfulness and joy of life with both.

I quote Unamuno again, "To believe in God is, in the first instance, to wish that there may be a God, to be unable to live without Him." Whence comes this intense desire for faith? When desire for human hunger sweeps us, we find therein food to satisfy us. When desire for human love comes over us, we find there is such a thing in the world as human love which meets our needs. But why should we be born with this equally intense hunger for faith, unless there were something in this universe to correspond to it, to meet and satisfy it?

THE second step in finding faith is to go where faith is. If you wanted to raise a garden of roses, you would not go into the arctic regions to do it, but to a temperate climate, where roses flourish. If you want an education, you can stay at home and get it by correspondence, but the normal thing is to go to school or to college. You can, and some do, find faith in a vacuum, by yourself, by thought, and suffering, and observation. But a much more natural process is to go where people have faith and consort with them and see how they got it.

That is where the church comes in. All of us who love the church are aware of her human defects: we are all apt to see the hole rather than the doughnut. But be practical— do you think the Christian religion would have survived the shocks and storms of nineteen centuries, none worse than the present tornado of Communism, unless it had been organized, bound together in a body, a body of people charged with keeping the faith intact and spreading it as far as possible? We haven't done all we should, and are not doing it now; but what is being done, is being done mostly by the Christian church.

There is more faith and more consecration than we think in the church. Christ gets to people more truly than some of us believe. Often we do not take them one-half far enough; we are content with defective commitment and consecration, but God gets through in spite of us sometimes. The normal, natural way by which people come to faith is through the fellowship charged with keeping and spreading the faith; and that is the church.

What we are saying is that faith comes through fellowship. The organized church, with its ordered worship and clear-cut beliefs, declares its faith, not only every time it says the Creed, but almost every time it worships. One of the best and wisest things about the church is the way we learn our faith by expressing it in worship. But what about people who hitch on this point or that? Or who just feel skeptical and can't accept these things? I believe that the church must break down its large fellowship into smaller fellowships, in which people can gather informally and air their questions and hear from others how they resolved their doubts and came to believe.

Some of us who work on college campuses know how effective it is to get undergraduates together in small companies, have someone witness in a clear, simple way to what Christ means to him and is doing for him, and then have what undergraduates often call a "bull session," where those who believe carry on a kind of friendly strife with those who do not—where doubts and difficulties are aired, and often resolved, not only by good reason, but by the unmistakable evidence of lives in whom Christ is a reality and a power.

The church must learn how to set in motion these informal companies, which both initiate and conserve spiritual belief and experience. It is often the most effective way to get others to believe. If we, and later they, come in contact with people who have faith, and can give good evidence for why they believe, based on experience, we shall find faith very contagious.

We who believe and are already in the church must be very sensitive always to those who come to church, and may be sitting beside us, who do not yet believe in any strong, effective way. We must use our imaginations and put ourselves back in the day when faith was very fresh and new to us. And if we were brought up in it (as I was), we must learn how to understand those who were not, and not put them off by giving them the impression that we think ourselves superior to them because we have always gone to church!

ANOTHER thing that can help faith immensely is the right kind of reading and study—the New Testament, first and foremost, of course. Begin reading the epistles, perhaps in a modern translation, and see what the Early Church thought about who Jesus was and what was central in this Christian faith. Then go back and read the gospels, in the light of this, to discover the nature of His human life. Dr. Charles Whiston's book, *The Ministry of Jesus*, will help you in this. For those who want to start the faith-experiment, I frequently recommend any of Dr. Frank Laubach's books on prayer.

THE FOURTH thing that helps us find faith is to begin the spiritual experiment in our own lives. You begin it exactly like you begin an experiment in physics or chemistry. You hear that if you mix two ingredients, a certain result will happen. You try it for yourself. If you are seeking a discovery that has not been made, you must take some hypothesis as being true, act as if it were true, and see what happens.

The experiment of faith is just as simple, as accessible, as law-abiding as that. Begin reading your Bible. Begin going to church. Begin acting as if God were, by praying. If you feel doubt, tell Him so. Be honest. Call on Him when first you awaken in the morning. Say over the old familiar things like the Lord's Prayer. Ask Him to use you this day, to guide you in working out the solution to your problems, the knotty ones as well as the rest.

A man was telling me the other day about a complicated and difficult business situation he faced. One night from nine till three he sat down to write out what he thought was the solution. He said it "came" to him that what he was writing was not quite just his own words and thoughts. He let God work in the situation by being open to Him, praying and working at the same time. Try that. Go as far with it as you can. Behave and live as if God were, and you will find that He is. Reach out to Him in every way open to you, and He will make Himself known to you. Try and continue to try the spiritual experiment.

And then act. Carlyle reminds us, "Doubt of any sort

cannot be removed except by action." Not much will happen when you remain on dead center—get off dead center, and follow the line of the best light you have. Do the obvious right thing, and then God can lead you to the inspired thing. Get in motion. You can't guide a bicycle leaning against a wall—you can only guide a bicycle that is in motion. God cannot guide a person who always stands still, paralyzed by doubt and misgiving. Better step out and make a mistake, and really get in motion—then God can get at you to correct the mistake.

FAITH is not faith in a static God, but in a dynamic God. Our religion is not just a set of theological or moral propositions in which we believe. Our religion is a stream of grace and power flowing out from God, to us, and then through us. When we get into that stream, we are carried along by it. It bears us and lifts us and moves us and guides us. But we must commit ourselves to it, and immerse ourselves in it.

Some of us in the Church are just decorously looking on, watching a process that takes place in some people's lives but not our own. We are like Alexander Woolcott, who was very fat. He said concerning the great virtue of work, "I admire work like everything; I can sit and watch it by the hour."

Faith does not believe in a God who just "exists," as I may believe that an equestrian statue exists in a city in South Africa; faith believes in a God who lives, and loves, and reaches out to man, and down to him, helping him with his life, guiding him in the way he reacts to difficulties, strengthening him where he is weak and using him—when he is open

—to serve His great divine ends and purposes. Real faith begins when we surrender ourselves to that God who manifested Himself in Christ, giving as much of ourselves as we can to as much of Him as we know. When we try that experiment, we shall feel ourselves "met," as the Quakers sometimes say. We shall know that God is.

You may know the witness of Horace Bushnell. When he was young and unbelieving, but wanted to find God if He existed, he says he "prayed to the dim God, confessing the dimness for honesty's sake." And he says he arose from his knees saying, "A Being so profoundly felt must inevitably be." He became, of course, a great Christian and Christian leader. May that doorway of discovery be one that some of you enter today to find what he found!

3.

The Way of the Cross

The Secret of Christian Discipleship

DURING LENT, as we recall the outstanding events of Jesus' life, we remember His so-called "triumphal entry" into Jerusalem. His ministry had mainly been exercised in the North, but He was driven by an inward urge to go to Jerusalem and to ask for a verdict from the people. He had made His way down the Jordan valley and was lodging in Bethany. On "Palm Sunday" He came to the city.

Falling in with an ancient prophecy, He rode upon a donkey. And the people threw palm branches in His path as He neared the city. They were enthusiastic about Him in a shallow kind of way.

Already there was mutiny in His own company. Judas knew the hostility both of the Jewish religious authorities and the Roman political authorities, and his disloyalty was already formed in his mind. In five days Jesus would be dead, crucified by the kind of organized religion and totalitarian political despotism which then thrived in Palestine. The triumph of this day was short-lived, just as you sometimes sense, when the sun is shining, that clouds will soon come over and obscure it.

How would you and I have felt, if we had been part of that little apostolic company that traveled with Him, and been quartered around at different houses of friends of Mary and Martha and Lazarus in Bethany? This Man had come on the scene of our lives and changed everything. We saw in Him such life as we had never seen before—such beauty, such power, such sheer spiritual principle, such an amazing way of touching people's hearts. It was all so good—nothing to regret, or be disturbed about.

But then He began talking about going to Jerusalem. And sometimes He said He would be betrayed into the hands of wicked men, and be crucified. Simon Peter dared to tell Him this would never happen to Him, and He told Simon, "Get behind me, you Satan; your outlook is not God's but man's."

As time went on, the whole thing grew more ominous. The clear skies and friendly response of Galilee gave way to the overhanging clouds and mutterings of some in Judea. The whole thing began to look bad to them. He had only been at work for two-and-a-half or three years—His work was hardly started—and here He was talking about being crucified. Couldn't He soften it down a little, take another course, avoid the needless shame and failure of the cross? That was how they felt, and how we would have felt.

But Jesus saw deeply into the workings of the law of God, His Father, in His world. Something in Him told Him that this had to be done; there was no other way. The course for Him was not to avoid the cross, but to make the cross work for His supreme end, namely the building of His Kingdom in the world through the hearts of men. This drew a minus sign right across His own life, cut Him off in His prime, blew Him out like a candle. Humanly it looked like the height of folly. Spiritually He believed it the only way.

In the twelfth chapter of John's gospel, Jesus gives His philosophy of the cross. And this is the heart of it: "Except a grain of wheat fall into the earth and die, it abideth by itself alone; but if it die, it beareth much fruit. He that loveth his life loseth it; and he that hateth his life in this world shall keep it unto life eternal."

What long-range wisdom, and yet what an assignment for His friends! To think that they were part of the spearhead of the greatest spiritual awakening that had ever come to their people, and the whole thing was to go up in the smoke of failure! He took it calmly, and saw in it the outworking of God's laws. They took it with horror, and saw in it the failure of their Leader.

We understand them; we would have felt as they did in their situation. But their wishing it away did no good. The cross came, and He died. And God raised Him up. He lost His life, and kept it unto life eternal.

This is a side of Christianity we generally like to avoid. We love it up in Galilee, where Jesus is talking about the lilies of the field and becoming like little children; but we did not know we were in for any crosses. Why can't people simply be kind to each other, we say, "live and let live," follow out Jesus' moral ideals and have everything come out all right?

We do not know what we say. The reason why this shallow, man-made religion is insufficient is because there is evil at large and at work in this world and universe. You cannot dab some salve on a cancer and expect a cure. You cannot heal what Jeremiah called "the hurt of my people" by any such light remedy as that. The heart of the evil in the world is in the "prince of darkness" and in the sin of man. Our rebellion against God, our misuse of the freedom He gave us, has thrown the universe itself into confusion. So vast an evil needs a vast cure. A little kindness and a few high ideals will not do what needs to be done—much more is required.

MAN needs redemption from his sins and the wreckage he has caused by them. We are not part of a nice, neat creation, set in motion by a loving God; we are part of a mutinous world where rebellion against God is the order of the day, not alone in millions of human beings (and to some extent in every one of us), but in that fallen angel, Satan, who is the leader of the works of darkness, the arch-fiend who inspires the evil that is in the world. No religion is of any practical worth, nor capable of permanence, which does not recognize this terrible malignancy in the universe.

Shallow, soft religion, with comfort and prosperity as its objectives, is not only inadequate in such a world; it is treasonable. For the great warfare is between God and all that rebels against Him. To deny the war is traitorous as to fight on the wrong side. Life is worse and more tragic than many of us like to admit. The joy which God gives us in the Christian adventure is the joy of knowing Him, of being with Him on the side that must eventually win, the joy of battle itself; it is not the joy of easy complacency and thinking everything is all right. The cross is God's sign that everything is not all right, and is only right at all because He has provided a way of reconciliation with

Himself which is the first step in personal and world redemption.

The cross is primarily about that. The first thing man needed was to be set right again in his relations to God. Man cannot do that by himself. He cannot repent himself back into fellowship with God. He is too far gone for that. It would only minister to his pride and self-satisfaction if he could heal his own predicament. Only God can deal with the mutinous sin of man.

The basic problem of the atonement is one you meet every time you try to deal with a real wrong in your own child. You want him to say he is sorry; then you want him to know he is forgiven, not by you only, but by God. Yet this must be done in such a way that he does not ignore the moral law, or think forgiveness comes easily. Even God will not forgive in such a way as to belittle the moral law.

Therefore God comes into life Himself, takes upon Him the burden of human sin, and dies a human death upon the cross, that men may see the cost of forgiveness—may realize that they are forgiven, yet in such a way that God's moral law is upheld and vindicated. God had to do this for us if it was to be done; and He did it.

Now Christianity, the religion of Jesus, teaches that we must first accept this great redemption; and then ourselves follow in the way of the cross. How lightly do we sometimes take those words, as we hang a little cross of gold unthinkingly about our necks! How few of us enter into what Jesus meant when He said, "Except a grain of wheat fall into the ground and die, it abideth by itself alone; but if it die, it beareth much fruit." We do not want to die. We want to live—richly, interestingly, profitably in this

The Way of the Cross [35]

world—to make our mark, to enjoy our comforts, and to do a little good conveniently on the side.

Did Christ not say He had come that we might have life and have it more abundantly? Yes, He did; and that is what He came for. The question is how we find that life. He says, "He that loveth his life loseth it; and he that hateth life in this world shall keep it unto life eternal." We want to take one easy leap upward from life to super-life. He says we must do it in two steps. The first is the step downward into death, and the second is the step upward into super-life. He wants us to have the super-life. He wants us to find our life and keep it unto life eternal, but the way of the Christian is the way of the cross. His method of finding super-life is to die to self.

And we do not usually die to self by creating deliberately a situation in which we make this decision. We usually have it forced on us by life. A great hope goes by the board, and life seems bereft. We lose someone who is dearer than life itself. Our sins and the cruelty with which others meet them reduce us to humiliation. We are confronted with a decision which puts Christ and other people first and runs the same minus sign through our own selves as the cross ran through Christ.

How we should like to evade these things! What would we not give to run away, or anaesthetize ourselves against them by pleasure, travel, even the indulgence of grief— anything to avoid the sharp pain of the cross! But there the situation is, facing us as the cross faced Jesus that Palm Sunday. Somehow He knew God was in that cross. He determined not to run away from it, but to see in it God's laws fulfilling themselves.

He put aside all thought of Himself, and committed Himself again to God and His work in the world. "And I, if I be lifted up from the earth," He said, "will draw all men unto me." His greatness, His effect in the world, would not come by seeking greatness; it would come by sacrifice. He knew He would matter more to men crucified on a cross than He could matter in any other way.

That is the characteristic Christian faith. Commenting on the various basic ideas of the different religions, a world missionary once made a valuable summary, which goes as follows: Greece said, "Be moderate; know thyself." Rome said, "Be strong; order thyself." Confucianism says, "Be superior; correct thyself." Buddhism says, "Be disillusioned; annihilate thyself." Hinduism says, "Be separated; merge thyself." Mohammedanism says, "Be submissive; bend thyself." Modern materialism says, "Be industrious; enjoy thyself." And modern dilettantism says, "Be broad; cultivate thyself." Christianity, on the other hand, says, "Be Christ-like; give thyself."

Now, in that giving of self—which really means dying to self—we find ourselves. We come to believe this by looking in two directions: first, at the person who ignores this law completely, and goes on the other principle of "loving his life." Jesus says he "loses" it. Watch the curve of the life of the selfish man. Watch him picking his selfish way through life's responsibilities and difficulties, till he comes to a lonely old age. You just can't win that way in a universe that runs by God's laws—the laws which Christianity reveals.

And we come to believe it, second, by looking at those who follow this law completely, and "hate" their lives in this world, in the sense that they are not out to succeed or to have power or to amass a fortune, but only to do the will of God. Watch them make the unselfish decision, let the minus sign cancel them out, take the way of the cross. And then watch the fruits and the results, and hear men rise up in the end to call them blessed. And better yet, hear God's voice saying, "Well done, good and faithful servant. . . ."

One takes the way of the cross because it needs to be taken. A Schweitzer goes to Africa because white men have ill-used black men, and black men are in need.

But there is another consideration here. Our world is in a precarious state. We hardly know from week to week where we stand, or what a day may bring forth. We like to think that all the evil of the world is concentrated in the Kremlin, and I for one believe it an outpost of hell, with demonic power possessing its leaders and their followers. But who of us, and what nations of the world, have not had a hand in making today's world? Half of America is avowedly godless. Much of the Christian Church is half-hearted. Our real hearts are in money and power and success.

All materialism is of one piece; Russian materialism and American materialism are sisters under the skin. If you ride the democratic way because it brings you what you want, and they ride the communistic way because it brings what they want, what is the difference between you in your basic values? But if you make your democratic way the footnote to the Christian way, then you are in a different column.

No man knows what we are in for, as a result of our sins. God lets crisis confront the world, and war if necessary, so that men will learn His laws. If they will not learn and obey them voluntarily, then they will have to learn and obey them involuntarily. God will deal with men by love if possible, but by judgment if necessary. Let us not be surprised nor unduly alarmed if we reap the results of thinking we could have peace by wishing for it, when we know that the only coin that will buy peace is righteousness and justice. We shall learn it in the end, if humanity must go through another war to learn it.

When man voluntarily takes the way of the cross, the way of sacrificing self, of giving self, for God and for others, then he will not have the way of the cross of war thrust upon him. We must learn that the way of the cross is written into the constitution of this universe, and it is the only way that leads to life and to peace.

4.

How to Know the Will of God

Finding God's Plan Daily

THE MOST DEDICATED and directed and inspired people in the world seem to feel that God has had something to do with what they are doing. They have felt impelled to do it, and they have felt guided in it. This may be called wishful thinking and self-deception, or it just may be that these people have discovered the new dimension which all men really seek and need.

But how does this happen? Why do some men experience it, while others drift idly and aimlessly, pursuing false or half-worthy ends? Is it that some are truly inspired? Or is it just that some have sufficient egotism to think that God is concerned about them? Only those who have had the experience can tell us, or serve as adequate samples of the human experience which in the end alone convinces.

Let us begin with the Apostle Paul. Three times in the Book of Acts the story of his conversion is given, twice in the first person singular. In his account in Acts 22, he asks two profound questions after Christ had met him on the Damascus Road. The first is, "Who are you, Lord?" The second, "What shall I do, Lord?"

They are in the right order. We must first discover with whom we are dealing. The Person whose disciples Saul was persecuting suddenly met him face to face. He was pretty sure who it was, but he had to ask the question: "Who are you?"

So must we. Before we know what He wants us to do, we must settle who He is.

Is Jesus Christ just another human leader, Himself seeking God and trying to draw people to Him—or is He the divine Son of God, the world's Saviour, as He claims? He certainly believed this of Himself, and let others believe and say it of Him. If in Christ God spoke finally to the world, we need look no further. Here is our truth and our anchor.

To know the will of God, we must know God. And we only really know God as He manifested Himself in Christ.

SOMETIMES we get impatient. Having ignored God while the sun was shining, we come running to Him when the clouds gather, saying, "What shall I do?" I think He says something like this:

"Get quiet for a while. You have been feverishly pursuing your own will for a long time. Before I can tell you what to do, you must let Me come into your life, not just for occasional help, but for good and all. Do you really want to know My will, and do it, or do you want Me to sanction your will, and help you get what you want?"

We must find God before we seek God's will.

How to Know the Will of God [41]

Also we may find that we must attend to some other things before we get the answer to the question that is on our minds. We who have been quite indifferent to God's will suddenly become very insistent about it. We think the answer to a problem is the priority. God knows that the priority is to get us where He can talk to us, about it and also about everything else.

The first thing Christ said to Saul, after Saul said, "What shall I do, Lord?" was, "Rise, and go into Damascus, and there you will be told all that is appointed for you to do." There was an intermediate step before he could take action in finding God's will.

What was in Damascus? Well, the people he was persecuting were there. He was going to have to hear and learn something from other Christians, and I suspect he was going to have to tell them in all honesty how terribly wrong he had been.

Not long ago a young man was seeking sincerely for more spiritual power in his life. It came to him that this could not happen till he went to a couple in his church from whom he felt estranged and apologized for his own wrong in the situation.

Many of us are in a stew about the big questions of life in which we do not know the will of God, because we do not first go and clear up some other situation, where we know the will of God very well. We shall find that we can't seek the will of God in some areas, but only in all.

With these indispensable preliminaries cared for—our initial commitment to God, and our seeking to clear up something clearly wrong—how do we discover what God wants us to do? In one way, it would take omniscience to answer that question. But for all of us it seems that there are some very clear steps:

We must ask God in prayer, "What shall I do, Lord?" Now there are some kinds of "prayer" that are not really prayer at all. There is the fevered asking on the part of someone all tense and tight inside, to whom nobody, not even God, can get through. There is the wilful, insistent asking for God to bless what we want to do; and that is not prayer. We cannot pray at all until we realize that often God must say to us, "My thoughts are not your thoughts, nor My ways your ways."

If you like your own way as much as I do, you will often find a cross at the heart of this procedure, for God must run a minus sign right through the upstanding I and cross it out before He can tell me what He wants. To ask for God's will is to want His will instead of our own. We must relinquish our will to find His. "Not my will, but Thine be done." Praying includes an openness to Him and His will.

In this connection, let me draw your attention to one of the great "opening" texts in the Bible—one that you may find infinitely productive and fruitful in your experience, as I have in mine. It is John 7:17, "If any man wills to do His will, he shall know. . . ." The verse says he shall know "of the doctrine" or the teaching. We cannot understand what the theology of Christianity is about until our lives are aligned with God's purpose. But this goes further: we shall not know what God's purpose is until we are aligned with it.

When men climb an unclimbed mountain, they can choose their objective, but they can hardly know the path till they set out. The destiny indicates only the direction of the path, not its outlines. But, in this case, the summit

How to Know the Will of God [43]

may be shrouded in cloud. You will not know what God's will is until you accept it, sight unseen.

Do you know that on August 23, 1864, Abraham Lincoln wrote a resolution on a piece of paper, which he folded, and asked his cabinet to endorse with their signatures without reading it? They did so, committing themselves blindly to whatever he had resolved. Exactly so does God ask us to affix our signatures to His will, as yet unknown.

PRAYER includes all of this. Prayer seeks God's will, not its own. Prayer sets the mind and will to obedience. Through such obedience we learn to know what God's will is. We pray as often as we can remember to pray, and whenever we have a moment in which to do it. Underlying and running through all our prayers of whatever kind, must be this one big one, "What shall I do, Lord?"

Don't pray to escape trouble. Don't pray to be comfortable in your emotions. Pray to do the will of God in every situation. Nothing else is worth praying for.

We do not command the will of God. But it may be that on the street, or in the midst of working at something else, there will come a luminous thought, or a resolution of conflict. Scientists have this happen when they discover the answer to a problem they have been wrestling with. Artists often feel it when that inspired phrase of music, or sweep of the brush, "comes" to them. The self-evident authenticity of what is thus revealed, adjudged either by inherent truth, or by practical consequences, will confirm the rightness of what has been given us.

We need a good measure of thinking and common sense in knowing the will of God. Experience bears upon the rightness of our perceptions. The counsel of wise people will help us, if they themselves are wise with God's wisdom, and not just the wisdom of this world, which is often long-run foolishness. A good many of us who call ourselves Christians are about ninety-five per cent worldlings with one eye on the conventions of religion, and in no danger of going off the deep end with religious enthusiasm. But all who take religion seriously must learn how partial are our insights, and how prone to self-deception and rationalization we all are. We need to learn as many facts as we can concerning any situation.

Meanwhile, you cannot stop living. Go ahead and make the immediate decision as best you can. Obey what you know, that you may learn what you do not yet know. Be as obedient as you can about the routine decisions that have to be made. Pray as often as you can. Try to draw your life more under the canopy of God's will.

When you must finally make a decision about the point at issue, make it without fear. With all the light you have, step out in faith, and *act*. You may not find out, as Drummond says, till afterward, perhaps long afterward, that you have been led at all!

Dr. Karlis Leyasmeyer told some people in Pittsburgh that there are three tests for finding out whether a course of action is God's will:

(1) *Test it* by the revealed will and plan of God, as we know it in the New Testament. The more we know our Bible, the better will be our contact with Christ, and hence our knowledge of His will.

(2) *Pray about it*, and be ready for an answer. It is possible for us to have halted and wavered so long

that we need to give ourselves a push to recognize and accept the guidance God is giving us.

(3) *Test it by circumstances.* Does God offer you a stumbling block, or an open door? Sometimes God wants us to break through obstructions to find and do His will; but sometimes events positively conspire to make it known to us, and God is in the events.

Too many of us fail to pray for God's will in small things—the things of daily routine. He can and will warn us against wrong courses, or wrong ways of taking the right course. The habit of saying a hundred times a day, "What shall I do, Lord?" instead of telling God what you want Him to do for you, will lead to a life lived under Him, with Him, and for Him.

At times there are big decisions—marriage for the young, occupation, a change of residence, or retirement for the older. "What shall I do, Lord?" He has a plan. If we seek it, we shall find it. He "has a way of letting us know it."

May I be quite personal here, and tell you what factors entered into my own decision to accept the invitation to a new church some years ago? That was one of those major decisions—at least for me. A committee came to New York and offered me the call to Calvary Church in Pittsburgh. They spoke of the great physical advances and improvements in Pittsburgh and said there needed to be a corresponding advance spiritually. This sounded exactly right, as the way to think about a new rector. But I felt as if they were talking about someone else, not me. Not only did I feel they were looking for something too big for me to deliver, but it had at that time no "pull" for me. I felt like a hypocrite, taking their time and eating their lunch!

I had been in my New York parish for nearly twenty-seven years. The roots were deep; why dislodge them? I like to pioneer and strike out in new directions, but I am conservative about my roots and base of operation. A work wider than parochial had been built up there.

But then, I thought, a man can stay too long, and the parish becomes too much identified with him. I knew Pittsburgh was a magnificent opportunity. I knew and loved Bishop Pardue. As I weighed the facts, they seemed about equal for staying or leaving. As yet I felt no guidance in the matter—and time was running on and before long I must make a decision.

One morning my wife and I were having our devotions in our room, and she said to me, "Are you really praying about that Pittsburgh call? I think it might be from God, and not just from Pittsburgh." She went out of the room to take our younger daughter to school. And then I said to the Lord, out loud so I wouldn't have any doubt about it, "Lord, do You want me to go to Pittsburgh? Because if You do, I'll go."

Then something indicative happened. Sometimes He guides in words, sometimes in pictures. I saw a stone block come lose in a wall, with the cement broken and dry around it, and up-end itself. So help me, it seemed to lean in the direction of western Pennsylvania. I went downstairs for breakfast and into the study, and tackled my mail. A little later I was musing to myself about something that was going to happen the next autumn. And something said to me, "There's not going to be any next autumn for you here."

I never could get that stone to go back in place, nor escape the conviction that God was showing me His will. I never had three seconds of doubt that it was His will for me to go. And the wonderfully encouraging things that took place since have only deepened the sense that God was in that decision.

I tell this, partly because it is good for ministers to let people know they experience the same perplexities as everyone else, but also because I want to point out how very uncertain I was for a time, and how very certain it seemed to be in the end. I say this to encourage you to believe that when you say to God from your heart, "What shall I do, Lord?" He will, in His own time and way, answer your prayer with unmistakable guidance.

5.

God and War

The Real Conflict in the World

I BELIEVE IN GOD. I believe that the uniformity of natural law, and the sublime compulsions of moral law, point to unity and purpose in creation itself. This means that intelligent planning is behind it, which must come from one Mind. All things have sprung from the mind of God. He creates, sustains, and orders all things. He created men to be the objects of His love, and He reveals to us His nature and character in Jesus Christ.

You ask, "How can you believe in a God of love when you know that men are dying horrible deaths every day, that women and children are undergoing unbelievable cruelties and suffering, that half of humanity is an armed camp against the other half?"

My instant reply is that I did not wait for war to come along to begin thinking about the problem of evil. The war is only a part of the whole problem of evil which has been here from the beginning and will be here till the end. Evil is just as present, qualitatively, in a single murder as in a war. Pain is just as terrible, just as painful, seen in the accidents of a great city, or in those suffering on beds of pain at home, as in any area of the war. Most of us have never considered these things until they were repeated on such a huge scale that we had to consider them because there were so many of them. If we had been mature Christians, we would have faced evil already in very concrete form. We would have seen that it attacked and destroyed Jesus Christ on the cross. That should have made us face the problem of evil long ago.

Now in considering the problem of evil, we must go back to what kind of a world God wanted to make. If He was to make a world which had any moral significance, it had to be a world in which there was moral choice. And if it was to be a world with moral choice, it had to be a world in which there was freedom. And if it was to be a world with freedom, then it had to be a world in which men were really free to choose good or evil. God Himself, it seems to me, was up against the choice of either making a world that was perfect but morally meaningless, in which men would be like fine statues—or of making a world that was imperfect but morally significant, in which men would be like growing children. That was a risk. If a man has a real opportunity to spend his life selfishly, and a real opportunity to spend his life unselfishly—that is, if he is really free to choose—he may make the wrong choice. He may choose to live selfishly, which upsets things, both for himself, and for the world about him. He often thinks he can beat the game and cheat the universe.

But such a man finds out, sometimes at long last, that he cannot beat the game and cheat the universe. God has set certain limits to liberty by law. We are free to choose evil, and ever since Eden we have been doing so. But we are not free to escape the consequences of choosing evil.

God has let us know what He thinks of evil in two ways. First, He puts His moral law into our hearts, so that something in us distinguishes between good and evil the moment we see them.

And, second, He shows us His condemnation of evil by its consequences. Someone said that God damns evil by letting it work itself out. The point is this: when men have refused to cope with the evil which they could control by making finer choices every day about small and great matters, then there may come upon them a great, external evil which they cannot control. This is exactly what is happening to us today.

We all know, or ought to know by now, that there is an intimate and organic connection between the blessing of human freedom and the Christian religion. The belief that man deserves to be free arises out of the Christian concept of human life. The practical matter of making man decent enough to get free, and strong enough to stay free, is made possible by a power that changes and lifts human nature.

In this, Christianity has done more than any other force in history. There is obviously some connection between the great experiment in democratic liberty represented by the founding of this republic, and the fact that nearly every one of our founding fathers was a deeply believing and practicing Christian. Those men were not all saints, and the people who won our independence were not either, but they certainly held more firmly than many of us do to basic beliefs of the Christian faith.

God and War [51]

We also know that, almost ever since the generation of men who won our liberty was gathered to their fathers, our nation has been more and more concerned with the *rights* of liberty, rather than with its responsibilities. In a republic for which patriots risked and gave their lives, millions of their followers have not even been willing to risk the loss of a profit, or a business deal. They paid for liberty with what it took: we want it on the cheap. It was John Philpot Curran, an Irish wit and politician, who said in 1790, "The condition upon which God hath given liberty to man is eternal vigilance."

We often wake up to the need of vigilance too late. Vigilance means more than watching against political encroachments upon our rights. It means seeing to it that the soil and climate of liberty, which is the Christian outlook on life, are kept sweet and healthy. A man goes into a forest, makes a clearing for himself, builds his house and plants his garden; but unless he takes the axe to springing saplings and keeps his ground clear, the wilderness will come in and possess his ground again. He must always have his axe out. Just so must we always have our axe out, to cut down the things that encroach upon our Christian civilization.

We should, for instance, have seen long ago what would be the fruit of godless, humanistic education. You can't have your churches emphasizing faith and morals, your homes half-heartedly backing them up, and your schools telling your children that faith is superstition and morals a survival of tribal taboos, and expect to have citizens for America tomorrow who know what was the strength of America yesterday.

America can no longer straddle a Christian heritage and a pagan outlook. We have got to choose which we want.

Personal breakdowns and national dividedness of mind result from the present deadlock. We must go back to our Christian heritage in dead earnest, and so preserve our Christian freedom because we create men and women who know how to appreciate freedom. Or we must acknowledge frankly that we are a pagan country, and take the medicine that is being given on all sides to those who have lost the inner controls which make freedom practical, and so must suffer the outer controls which destroy it altogether.

This nation has had the greatest privileges ever given to any nation in all time. America has been God's privileged child. But America has become a spoiled child. We have been ungrateful to the God under whom our liberties were given to us. It is high time to say that war is God's judgment upon a godless and selfish people. We have been wicked, impious, and immoral. We have been in the hypocritical position of living off the blessings of our Christian past, while we ignored God's law, love, and church.

Because this went on without judgment for a time, we have kept it up—we began seeing how far we could go. But the God in whom we said we did not believe is showing us that we do not set aside His immutable laws by our unbelief. We shall find God, in Christ, in conscience, in the Church; or we shall find Him in chaos, in conflict, in catastrophe. But God is God, and He will not revoke His laws.

During the war there appeared in a newspaper in Bournemouth, England, the following sentences:

> We have been a pleasure-loving people, dishonoring God's day picknicking, and bathing—now the seashores are barred; no picnics, no bathing.

God and War [53]

We have preferred motor travel to churchgoing —now there is a shortage of motor fuel.

We have ignored the ringing of church bells, calling us to worship—now the bells cannot ring except to warn us of invasion.

We have left the churches half empty when they should have been filled with worshippers—now they are in ruins.

We would not listen to the way of peace—now we are forced to listen to the way of war.

The money we would not give to the Lord's work —now is taken from us in taxes and higher prices.

The food for which we forgot to say thanks—now is unobtainable.

The service we refused to give God—now is conscripted for our country.

Lives we refused to live under God's control— now are under the nation's control.

Nights we would not spend in "watching unto prayer"—now are spent in anxious air-raid precautions.

WHOEVER wrote those words knew that there is such a thing in this world as retribution. We in America are still in a position to see and recognize the working of that moral law, if we will, and to cooperate with it instead of defying it. We must all see that there is an answer to the question, "How can you believe in a God of love?" The answer is, He created laws which we broke, and this brought judgment down upon us. We are not our own judges, but we are the deciders of whether we obey the law of God or repudiate it. War is the fruit of sin, and sin is the transgression of the law.

Jeremiah says, "Hear, O earth. Behold, I will bring evil upon this people, even the fruit of their thoughts, because they have not hearkened unto my words, nor to my law, but rejected it."

This brings matters back to the roots. This is not defeatism, but facing the real source of the trouble. The materialists who see no need for anything today except industrial production, and military might, do not understand either the genius of America nor the laws of God. God deals with nations as with men. Whatsoever they sow, that shall they also reap. As with individuals, so with nations: "To whomsoever much is given, of him shall be much required." This is inexorable law. Ignorance of the law excuses no man in court; it excuses no nation before the judgment-seat of God.

What hope, then, can be held out to us? Much hope, because God is a God of love, as well as a God of law. The cross of Christ is the supreme revelation of Him; and there He does not set aside His law, but He takes its suffering consequences of our guilt upon Himself in our behalf. There He made atonement for the sins of men. This means hope, for it means redemption.

We have the opportunity to repent. It is not too late—it is never too late, whatever the consequences of our sins may still do to us. While we go to the fields and seas of battle, and while we go to the farms and factories to produce needed materials, there is another place where we need to go, and that is to the House of God, and to our knees.

ANY armament that does not include repentance is a shallow and inadequate armament, and it cannot defend us in the last analysis. I can think of no armament that man can create like the armament of a penitent, converted, praying nation. We have no right to pray to get off easily, or to evade the consequences of our sins in suffering; but we can pray to be forgiven, and we can pray for strength to do our duty under God. If it takes a great fear to bring a nation to its knees, then thank God for such a fear!

Also, in these days, God can and will give us the courage that we need. Remember that Christ never promised to anybody exemption from trouble and suffering. He only promised them strength to go through with it, without fear or bitterness. This nation is in real peril. All of us are in for loss, sacrifice, a changed way of life. How people expect to meet the ordeal that seems to confront us, simply in their own strength, I do not see. God gives men supernatural courage. We who know Him have an added strength, and an added responsibility; for many will look to us now to see if we behave differently, and "have something" which people without God do not have.

And lastly, let us never forget the sovereignty of God. He overrules all that man does, even his wickedness; and turns it all to His eternal purpose. He did not make life for us to be soft and easy, and we must never confuse human utopias of material ease with the kingdom of God. Christ and His apostles showed us life at its highest, and they were poor men, most of whom died violent deaths for their faith. Christ on His cross may be, not the interpretation of the hard places in life, but of life itself. And suffering love, the last word of reality.

When you put all this into a simple word we can all remember, it is the word of Paul, "All things work together for good to them that love God." All things—not some things; for good—not always for peace or pleasure; to them that love God—not to them that live without Him. God is at work today as always.

There are hinges in history, and we are at one of them now. But history does not come to an end; human life does not come to an end; and God does not come to an end. Above the long, tragic, glorious stream of human history is written the word that illumines it, that transfigures it, that justifies it—written as on the very heavens themselves: "Hallelujah, for the Lord God Omnipotent reigneth!"

6.

God and Peace

The Nature and Cost of True Peace

NOT LONG AGO a woman whom I know said to a friend of hers something about the need for God if we were to preserve peace. Her friend replied, "What on earth has God got to do with peace?" It is a good question, pretty far "up-stage," but that is where many people are.

I am sure that millions, if they said what they thought, would say the same thing. Peace, we are apt to think, means outmaneuvering a sly and convinced Soviet policy, and keeping the balance of world power in the hands of nations that, with all their faults, including the great fault of being willing to use peace sometimes to their own material advantage, at least do not provoke open wars in the world. What has God got to do with this?

Any of us, with the slightest acquaintance with history, knows also that it is not the way of God to destroy evil at its first appearance. History has seen many ruthless, unprincipled conquerors arise to plague and torture and exterminate their enemies. Only slowly does evil destroy itself by its own hateful unworkableness. Meanwhile, it goes on unchecked in a world where the Creator took the risks of endowing mankind with freedom.

The mills of God grind surely, but they grind slowly. God works through men, and that means slow progress. God does not often intervene in history with a providential lightning-bolt that destroys these destroyers of mankind. This time-lag in the workings of Providence permits every shade of skepticism and atheism to fill the minds of men, for we want to see peace come for no better reason than that it is more comfortable and more profitable.

What, then, has God got to do with peace? We all know that God gives peace in the heart, peace of mind. All who look facts in the face would allow that religious faith in God has given to men in all ages the greatest comfort that this world affords. By it they have stood uncomplainingly excruciating pain, "the slings and arrows of outrageous fortune," and long and sacrificial service for unprivileged people in foreign lands; and have gone through the losses, privations, and agonies of war itself without bitterness, hatred, or rebellion. We would all admit that God has something to do with personal peace.

But what about public peace—what about "world peace" —what has God to do with these? Can we ever expect Him to change His method of letting the tares grow together with the wheat till the harvest separates them in kingdom come? Can we look to God for any real help now, with the making of peace between nations? And if so, how?

GOD can help us to understand the nature of peace. Most people today, especially in our free countries where we have been spoiled and pampered with our blessings, think that peace is the natural right of every person, and war is an intrusion into their comfort and prosperity which ought not to occur. The Bible, however, takes a different view of peace. It everywhere looks upon peace as a resultant by-product of righteousness. Isaiah makes this clear in a number of places: "The work of righteousness shall be peace" (32:17); "There is no peace, saith the Lord, to the wicked" (48:22).

It seems to me there is no other boon which we men expect to have without working for it, except peace. We know that we cannot have education without working our minds, wealth without working our hands, desirable human relations without taking trouble for other people. Why should we expect to have peace without paying for it?

The coinage and cost of peace is righteousness. Just as you do not have peace of mind unless you are being the kind of person you should be, but acquire it as soon as you begin to become such a person, so the world itself does not enjoy peace until and unless it becomes the kind of world it should be. Insofar as it behaves and does the will of God, it enjoys peace.

It is amazing how little righteousness it takes to produce quite a lot of peace—as if God were leading us along like children, and showing us that this is the way. Peace therefore becomes, not the right of natural men, but the privilege of righteous men. Wicked men are always in broils with other men; wicked nations are always on the verge of war or in it. There is an everlasting connection between righteousness and peace.

But where is a man going to find this righteousness? The

truth is that when we come to look seriously for it, righteousness itself is also a by-product—it is a by-product of faith in God. Oh, you tell me, there are many righteous people in the world whose faith in God is very sketchy, perhaps non-existent. But have you thought of what it is they live by? Where did they get the ideals by which they live? Go back a generation or two and do you not find some rock-ribbed old grandfather, some gentle and believing mother, who lived in the climate of Christian faith? The next generation said, "We will get on without the faith, but we will keep the ideals." It was like saying we shall cut the roots off the flowers and keep the flowers, but cut-flowers will survive in water—for a while.

I know a magnificent woman with no faith. She is true, loyal, unselfish, and she got it from somewhere; but her children are a mess! She caught enough belief from somewhere to make her a fine person; she did not have enough to get it over to her children. One of them killed himself, and the rest have made havoc of their marriages.

Human idealism runs out. Its fountain is human lives, and they are limited, weak, and fallible. I believe a historic case could be made for the position that everything good in this world derived originally from people who looked above humanity for their final faith and sanctions. All our higher aspirations, then, derive from faith in God. That alone contends with the selfishness in man, calls him to account, and provides him with the inspiration that drives him on when righteousness is costly and calls for some sacrifice and austerity in our living.

Moreover, the righteousness which does not come from faith is soon found to come from pride. The person who sets out to become a "good" man or woman without the help or sanctions of God goes in one of two directions —success or failure. Insofar as such people fail to live up to their ideals, they become discouraged or despairing, self-centered and neurotic, tending to blame life, others, and circumstance for their failure. Insofar as they succeed (or think they do), they become self-satisfied, selfish, and proud.

If there be no God, or I ignore Him, and turn into what I think to be a quite estimable member of society, if I "live by the Golden Rule" or fool myself into thinking I do, because I so often say it, I inevitably become a self-satisfied individual. When something wonderful happens, to whom shall I turn to say thank you? To my own royal ego, of course—where else can I turn? If I fail and know that I fail (know it in my heart even if I will not acknowledge it), then I am eaten up with self-pity. I have nowhere to seek forgiveness unless I can manage to beseech the royal ego for forgiveness—and if I can get the ego to do it, I am happy on two counts: I am free to go ahead without guilt, and I have the almighty ego's approval.

We all know this is an elaborate scheme of make-believe, without moral, spiritual, or psychological foundation. We know that it underlies nearly all the broken human relations and the mental and nervous breakdowns of our time—and its damnation is principally its own utter impracticality.

Therefore God provided another kind of righteousness —not one that man creates and preserves for himself, but one that God provided for him in Christ. The righteousness arises not out of self-effort, but out of our faith in Christ—faith being, as it were, the wire along which our prayer travels to Him, and His power travels to us. If there be one thing in you and me that is "good," it is not our achievements which are always partial and limited, and not our characters which are a combination of good and evil, but our faith which aspires to God, and our intentions which would seek conformity to His will.

This "derived" righteousness is a favorite theme of the Apostle Paul, and has been part of the true and regal stream of Christian faith from the beginning. There is a washed-out echo of Christianity abroad today, containing nothing but assent to Christian ideals, that is no part of Christianity, for its base is pride and self-effort, instead of grace and faith. The only safe righteousness, the only kind that will not get off on lines of pride and complacency, such as mark not only most of those who profess to be good people without the help of God, but also many of us in the churches who are very little farther along than they, is this derived righteousness.

Jesus Himself is utterly central to this faith and righteousness. In a mighty word, best translated I think by Dr. Moffatt, he says, "It was in Him that the divine fullness willed to settle without limit, and by Him it willed to reconcile in His own person all on earth and in heaven alike, in a peace made by the blood of His cross." All of God is in Jesus, "the divine fulness without limit." "All redemption for man is in Jesus," reconciled in His own person.

All men must find and can find this salvation, "all on earth and in heaven alike." And all peace is the fruit of the cross, "a peace made by the blood of His cross"— not only our peace with God in atonement, but our peace

God and Peace [63]

with one another as the recipients of this so great salvation. In Jesus this vast, unique stream of blessing began pouring out of heaven down to earth. It gave man new hope and new life, and has gone on doing so, the one light in all the darkness of human life for nearly twenty centuries.

Many have been the by-product blessings of this Christian stream. One of them is human freedom. Plato envisioned a better world, but slaves were the very paving-stones for its base. Individual life is cheap where Christ has not come; it is cheap where He has been and is no more. Personally I doubt if the whole humanistic movement toward freedom in the eighteenth century could have taken place without the centuries of Christian influence behind it, with its insistence upon the worth of man.

Politics simply does not think that way unless Christianity presses somewhere upon it; politics finds it too easy to grab power and enslave men for some immediate glorification of a man or a plan. Nothing keeps states from going in the totalitarian direction except the democratic will of the people, which will is kept alert and alive by Christian faith. When that lacks or lapses, they drop down into contentment, first, with state benefits and provision, then with state control and gradual enslavement.

Every blessing and benefit of our democratic way of life is directly or indirectly traceable to God through the Christian faith. Our free enterprise, our intellectual freedom to study as we will and speak as we think, everything that makes the common life of our people all comes from our Christian heritage. Your freedom, your fortune, your political rights, everything that you, on a materialistic basis, think makes your life worth while, is a product of Christian faith.

THE Church has not always been in the forefront of progress, but on the whole where the Church has gone freedom and the greater opportunity for all have gone with it. Therefore, if you believe the world cannot continue half-slave and half-free, your own interests are at stake in the spread of the church to the ends of the earth, and in its support at home. Your money is needed, but it is not enough. The American Revolution was not won by paid mercenaries; it was won by the life-blood of our own ancestors. The revolution in the world will not be won by your hiring substitutes; it will be won as you care, as you go, as you send your children, as you care more for the Christian enterprise than you care for your own business or your own life.

Do you know what those who see and realize this, and yet will do nothing about it—do you know what they are? Lately I have seen more than the usual number of American pagans—lovable people personally so many of them, but defeated, failing in their primary responsibilities and relationships, their lives often a tangled web of compromise and deceit, living off what others have done for them in the past, making the best of the good land in which we live and putting nothing back into it, hoping someone else will go on being responsible and unselfish, hoping the church on the corner will still be there for a fashionable wedding when the daughter steps off, or a pompous funeral when the old man dies, damning the selfishness of other people all the time—and these are the people who expect our statesmen to create peace on earth and good-will to men! Do you know what they are, these benefiters by our Christian civilization, who live like pagans themselves? They are the real traitors to the race.

They are the fifth column of the forces of slavery in the world. These nice, pleasant people who tell you they wouldn't harm a fly are one of the real subversive forces in our nation and the world today. If they and others go on as they are, they will make another war inevitable, for as peace is the fruit of righteousness, war is the fruit of sin. If in war-time you lie back and take it easy and play the black market and thrive by others' misery, you know what the world calls you. Well, war between atheistic materialism and Christian liberty is a long way from being won. The enemy is not all across the sea; all who live as if the world of spiritual indifference and material comfort were the real world, they are part of the enemy, too. And it is high time they realized that they are as dangerous as a footpad in the night, an arson-bug with fire round a gas-tank, or a maniac with an atom-bomb in an airplane.

Sometimes we never know what we have till we lose it. Maybe the only way God can speak to people like that is to let their sins work themselves out, to see all this we love in ruins, to know the desperation that Hiroshima and Nagasaki knew. Maybe only bombs will talk to people who no longer pay any attention to God.

The world was never before in such peril as now. The danger from Soviet Russia is greater than the danger from Germany in 1939, because there are so many thousands of people whose materialism and moral defeat find comfort in Communism, and whose bitter self-hatred would find a ghoulish satisfaction in seeing the world about them in torment. There is something not only immoral but insane in people sitting by in indifference, living along in selfishness, blocking any real foundation for peace, by the utter selfishness of their lives.

I deeply believe we shall have no peace whatever in the world, but instead war more frightful than the imagination can conceive, unless we have a Christian awakening of world proportions. It is no good to sit here and wish this might happen. Will you let it begin to happen in you? Will you take the following steps:

(1) Admit that all the decency you know and all the freedom you enjoy derive ultimately from God and that Christian civilization is at stake and in peril today as it has never been in peril before?

(2) Admit that the personal responsibility of ordinary men and women has kept the flame of faith and of freedom alive in the world till this day, and that this can never be left to leaders and governments alone?

(3) Admit that this puts it right back in your lap and mine, and calls on us to live different lives with God at their center from now on, through Christ as our Saviour?

(4) Recognize that the compromise, materialism, godlessness, selfishness of your life constitute sin of the blackest order, defy God, and betray men?

(5) Get on your knees now and tell God you are sorry for failing Him and humanity, and want to repent and believe the Gospel?

(6) Link yourself with other Christian people in

some church, put your weight behind its program, work and pray and give for Christian missions?

(7) Make right all wrongs you have done to others, put Christian standards into your business practice, and really do what you say you want others to do, live this thing out seven days a week?

7.

How to Witness

Making Faith Alive and Relevant

HOW CAN YOU and I, as Christians, make our faith alive and relevant to people about us today? That is the most pressing question that the Christian Church faces in our time.

Probably greater headway has been made by the churches than most of us think; but at best it has been a great deal less than we need. If this nation is to fulfill the role that destiny seems to have handed to us, we need God, we need Christian faith and consecration, and we need simple goodness and decency, as we never needed them before. The church must find ways of reaching the untouched.

Chesterton says we remain psychological Christians long after we cease to be theological ones. There is an immense reservoir of rudimentary, unlearned adherence to belief in Christian values, which needs to be tapped and can be tapped if we will learn how to do it.

There are many ways of doing this. If the church is on the job, it will draw some of these people through vital services; they will come once, perhaps for curiosity, or in some special need, and may remain to believe, to work and serve. Any national or world crisis will send many into our churches, at least for a time. Our people seem to be slowly learning that there is a connection between freedom as we enjoy it and faith as we have inherited it, and are acquiring a dawning realization that only in the climate of faith does freedom thrive.

Basically Communism, and all the lesser forms of materialism or of subversion which serve its own ends, are a kind of religion. No mere human ideals can stand against such force. Only a right faith can in the end conquer a wrong one. Some people are seeing this a little more clearly, and it makes them realize that the success of the Christian enterprise is more than a benefit to their immortal souls. It may mean the safety of their human hides and the future freedom of their children and grandchildren.

And then there are the great special efforts of men like Billy Graham, who stir up complacent church people as well as complacent pagans, and make religion again seem a thing of fire and tingling significance instead of a thing of tradition and dullness.

Yet we know it is not enough. We know we are not, ourselves, doing enough. We know we ought to be doing more. And the most effective thing we can do is to find a more vibrant faith ourselves and then try to get it over to our friends.

The minute anyone begins talking like this, someone says to himself, "The best way to do that is by example." And everyone knows that the best sermons some of us will ever preach, and the best witness we shall ever give, is to meet life and its crisis with courage and sweetness and forgivingness and integrity. . . . Our lives must try at least to measure up to our spoken convictions.

But there is a limit to this. A good life can testify to the belief in some kind of Higher Power. But for Christians the distinctive thing is not that there is a God and therefore we ought to live like brothers; it is that God came into the world in Christ, redeemed the world by His death, rose again from the dead, and is alive forever more. Christians come to God in and through Christ, because we believe that in Him God did historically those "mighty acts" which guarantee what kind of God He is.

I do not know any mere example that can quite tell people that we believe God spoke in Christ to all men forever, or that Christ is His incarnate Son, or that the cross saves you and me from sin, or that the Resurrection is the crowning article of faith for us Christians. I would be insolently conceited to think that my life could ever become good enough to mirror these things very clearly to other people. Yet they are the verities in which my faith stands.

As I cannot on my piano render anything but the echo and reminder of the symphony which the New York Philharmonic can really play, so my single example can be but the faintest echo of the profound harmonies of the Gospel. I cannot play what the Philharmonic can play, but I can tell other people about it and get them to listen for themselves. What I cannot be or reproduce adequately, I can nevertheless talk about and point to. It is so with Christ. My faith can go far beyond my life. I am ashamed at how little of my faith I put to work in my life, but I

How to Witness [71]

am not in the least ashamed of my Lord and of my faith in Him.

There is another thing. An example may inspire us, or it may cause us to say, "Oh, yes, he (or she) is like that. He is not troubled by temper or nerves or impatience or worry as I am; he is just a happier temperament." We admire him, but it may not occur to us that perhaps he had to fight for his serenity, and we might win it if we would do the same.

Let me give you what I think are some of the elements in a Christian witness.

CHRISTIAN witness is witness to Jesus Christ, mediated through an experience of Him which we have had. If you do not know Him, if you are not reasonably clear in your faith about Him, you cannot witness. You may be a good person, a good humanist, and you may exercise a quite good influence on people; but it is not Christian witness. We witness, as Christians, to a great, objective faith in Jesus as the Son of God and Saviour of the world, who redeemed us by His cross, who rose from the dead on the third day, and who is alive forever more at the right hand of the throne of God. We witness also to our own personal and subjective faith in Jesus, not alone in what He has done for the world, but what He has done for us.

All true witness, whether public preaching or private testimony, contains these objective and subjective elements. Paul shows this perfectly when he says, "In Christ God reconciled the world to Himself instead of counting men's trespasses against them; and he entrusted me with the message of His reconciliation." The objective thing was God's mighty work in Christ. The subjective thing was Paul's experience of Christ, and call to tell men about Him. It must come in the same way to us.

For this reason we shall alternate, in what we say to people, from what we tell them of Christ to what we tell them of ourselves. We are not as important as Christ, obviously; but the first real impression they get of Christ's power may be our witness to what He has done for us.

It is most often more effective to begin with our own experience of faith than with the elements of belief that comprise it. You stand talking with someone, perhaps at a party. You begin with chit-chat. If you are a Christian, even your chit-chat and your jokes are different from those of others. You are praying with the back of your mind. In your reactions to events or people, something slips in that intrigues the other person. The conversation becomes, not more serious, but more real. Be ready, if it is right, to break open your life and experience to this person—not all at once, trying a little at a time. Often the other person will respond in the same way. Dare to come out with your faith as it relates to what you are talking about, and its relevance will strike the other person.

I was impressed once, when reading over cursorily, at one sitting, the New Testament epistles, to see how often Paul speaks about himself. He is not afraid to say "I." He tells his readers what happened to him. He even defends and justifies himself again and again.

Experience is the constant supporter of belief and conviction. The great objective truths provide the substance of our convictions; but the subjective experience is what provides the initial interest most often for those to whom faith is not yet real.

Such conversation as this leads people on to open their hearts to us. Most people are dying to talk about themselves. If they do not find the right person to talk with, they will talk with the wrong one! Millions of conversations take place every day, in which people seek sympathy, self-justification, and flattery, when what they need is sympathy, understanding, and spiritual challenge.

We get a foothold in human lives by naturalness, by humor, by caring for people. We get leverage in those lives by knowing when to agree and disagree, and also *how* to disagree. Without being "preachy" we can get across a different viewpoint, a higher set of values, the presence of divine Power.

When confidence is established, then people often begin really to talk. React with confidence and leisure, not with fear and hurry. Get in a quiet place if you can. Get physically comfortable. Don't talk much—let them talk. Don't begin bringing your answer too fast, nor until the story is really out in the open. We do not help people by smothering them with witness. We help them by understanding with quiet listening.

In the conversation somewhere is "the end of a string" you can take hold of. Perhaps there is too much blame put on others, not enough on one's own reaction to others; or we need to put the old truth that there are always two things—what happens to us, and how we take what happens. We can't always change what happens, but we can always control how we take what happens.

You will have to witness, out of your own life and out of others whom you know. Somewhere Christ has given the answer to just such a problem as this person presents to you. You need to know many living stories of changed people, for these are the leaven and the seed which set about changes in others.

SOMEWHERE in life-changing conversations comes another step: whittling out the point of responsibility. This happens when the person you're talking with begins to see the sin in himself, not in the other person—the self-pity, or the need to forgive or ask forgiveness. There may emerge one, or two, or four, or six things that are definite and constitute the hindrances and sins. Remember them as you talk. And remember the great old truth that "we take hold of God by the handle of our sins." That is, God comes at the point of need.

There is no virtue in feeling generally sorry for our sins, but only in facing what they are concretely. The more specific we are about what has been wrong, the more will our decision for Christ have content to it, and not consist in an emotional turn to God which is soon forgotten.

THE step of decision comes next. Many have joined the Christian Church without a comprehensive, drastic, intelligent Christian decision. That is why our consecration is weak and our commitment wavering. When one sees his needs and sins, he must bring them to Christ for His forgiveness; but in order to be forgiven, the sins must be faced and surrendered. Often we must face them out with another person, as AA's do.

We must, at the same time, surrender ourselves—our

wills—to God. We know certain sins and needs that this act will mean we must discard. We know also that this is a kind of "step in the dark," for we are telling God we will do from now on as much of His will as we see.

People must be helped to see what the content of such a decision is for them, and then helped to make it. They must not just tell us about it, and then "shake on it"— the decision must be given to God only, though a human witness may help to enforce it. Prayer will be natural at this point, as a way to ask God's forgiveness on the past and His grace for the future.

You can never in this world do any human being a greater service than to help him understand the meaning of taking this all-important step of self-surrender. Thousands in our churches are dull and lack-lustre, grim and defeated, unhappy, and to all intents and purposes out of Christ, because no servant of His has ever lovingly and directly dealt with them on this level. The church today has no greater business than to train tens of thousands of its people to do this.

The crux of it will lie in whether you actually get at people's real sins and needs, and whether you bring them to real decision and surrender to Christ. They may not be able to make a statement that they understand the whole of the Christian faith as yet, but any honest person can begin the spiritual experiment by surrendering "as much of himself as he can, to as much of Christ as he understands." I know dozens—yes, hundreds—of laymen who are now doing this tremendous work of helping other people into Christian experience.

When we have met the person, developed a real relationship with him, heard the problem that is on his mind, helped him to turn the problem, his own reactions to it, and himself over to Christ in surrender—what then?

First, fellowship. A new-born child needs warmth, food, love, attention. Whoever helped him through to decision must stick by him for a time. As children get gas and colic, a reborn person has his ups and downs in the early stages of growth. A chance to meet with several others regularly will see him over the first stages.

He will also need to be brought into the full fellowship of the church. This will mean some systematic instruction, and the study of the right kind of books. He will come to know the power and value of worship. But, important as this is, none of it should be a substitute for being carried along by one faithful guide, and beginning to know well a small Christian company. One may be born into a big family, where there are innumerable aunts and cousins; but the immediate family is only father and mother and some brothers and sisters. The whole congregation is too big and too impersonal to do certain of these primary things.

Individuals and small companies are the secret of the awakening of our parishes. It takes meeting after meeting to get things ground into the bones of those who are converted — Christian ideas, Christian caring, Christian fellowship.

Second, they will need to form steady and adequate devotional habits. Prayer is a new experience. When shall they do it? How? With what help from books? Bible study must begin at once; but the most elementary instruction may be needed.

A fine young churchman in my parish, who had started on a vital spiritual pilgrimage, said to me, "I have never read nor heard the Bible outside of church." That will go for tens of thousands of our young people. Hand them a Bible, and they do not know where to turn. I suggested John 3, Romans 7 and 8, and Luke 12 and 15. But people need a plan—either a year-round lectionary, a plan to study a book at a time (which will require a commentary), or a topical study of, say, faith, or money, or prayer. We all ought to know, and have on hand, good books that help in this, books that initiate experience. I think a live church ought to have a book-stall, where vital books are on sale; and all of us ought to be book salesmen, who make them known to others. And if we can guide people to find, or form, a group in which they can pray together, this, too, will help them grow more rapidly.

THIRD, they must in turn become witnesses themselves. "Go home to thy house and to thy friends, and tell them what great things the Lord hath done for thee" was Jesus' first commission to one who had just met Him and been transformed. This will need humility and humor, but it will also need courage and increasing tact born of experience.

Those in AA make no bones about what kind of people they have been, and what has changed them; they talk at the drop of a hat. It is just as bad to get drunk on fear or resentment, or on sleeping pills, or gossip, or temper, as it is to get drunk on whiskey or gin. Thousands and millions more suffer from these than from alcoholism. We need an army of witnesses who know what has happened to them, and are not afraid to say what it is.

Christian witness only takes a true beginning of conversion, some imagination, and a little courage. Most people have it, if you know how to draw them out. Many will witness first through the technique they understand, businessmen through a new spirit in their offices, women through their homes, artists through their art, doctors through medicine. In each case the job is meant to be a kind of sacrament. But nothing takes the place of dealing with individual persons and helping them to find what you have found.

A few years ago a middle-aged couple were invited for dinner to meet a woman from out of town. She heard they were religious; she was a pagan and so expected a dull evening. What was her surprise when she met two very attractive people who interested her at once. After dinner she found herself sitting beside a gentleman with a delightful southern accent and a plentiful sense of humor. Finding him sympathetic, she poured out all her troubles. Her blood pressure was too high, and her hemoglobin was wrong, and everyone had mistreated her. Here was a sympathetic ear into which she could pour all her troubles. He listened for a while then he said, "Why don't you just turn all this over to God?"

"What did you say?" she replied.

"Why don't you turn all this over to God?" he repeated. Her surprise and annoyance were soon followed by renewed interest. They went on to talk of many things and spent a delightful evening.

When she got home, she found that this man and his

wife had a letter waiting for her. They said they were praying for her, and had sent her some small books to read. After reading the letter, she ripped open the package of books and began to read. It wasn't long before she knelt down beside her desk and gave her life to God. "Within twenty minutes it was all over," she says. The cocktails and sleeping pills, the holier-than-thou attitude toward others, the fears and the self-pity "just-went." There was immediate physical improvement. The blood pressure went down to 127 and the red blood-count up to 4,800,000! Then also began reality in prayer and worship and stewardship of her income, which was not large, but she began tithing at once with no suggestion from anyone.

She became a constant witness to others. Today she can go to a party, talk with her old friends, or with new ones, and before leaving have more than one ask, "When can I see you privately?" Her son, who stood near the top of his class at Yale for four years, has come into a profound experience of Christ, largely from seeing what happened to his mother, and is now in seminary preparing for the ministry.

So do the circles widen out, when God through you can get people changed enough to manifest the difference, to intrigue others about it, and to be able to tell them what has made the difference. This was true in the beginning, is true now, and will be true forever. The greatest argument and proof for the Christian religion is the men and women in whose lives it has wrought a change, and who have learned the profound art of making real to others the faith that has changed the very nature of life itself for them.

FAITH AND DOUBT

I think, as gazing in the endless sky
On clear and starry nights, ofttimes that I
Have felt a wonderment as wild and strange
As ever crossed the mind of infidel:
Felt faith as iron-strong, secure from change,
As e'er graced saint at prayer within his cell.

What then of life? Of God? Of heaven and death?
Our wonder may be mother to our faith.
Faith were not living, fresh and new and stout,
Were wonder never deep enough for doubt.

How to Witness [81]

8.

The Wonder of Forgiveness

"Good News" for Everyone

A LETTER FROM a friend in England says, "I would really like to talk with you about the curse of fear and guilt that lies like a cloud over people. Psychologists say that there is to be no more condemnation, but they don't see that Christ provided forgiveness so that the fog of guilt and fear could dissolve in the sunlight of God's forgiveness. What they do is to try and get rid of it by saying that people are wrong to feel it. Do you agree?"

I have never known such widespread anxiety, insecurity, and guilt as one finds in people today. Not only are there people who are emotionally and mentally sick with these things, but there are pockets of them in most normal people.

I have been trying to analyze what this extra amount of fear, guilt, and insecurity comes from. We realize the peril in which we find ourselves. The release of atomic energy hangs like a sword over humanity's head. We may be afraid as animals are afraid when they come near a slaughterhouse; maybe it is the impending danger that strikes terror to many hearts.

It is hard to be precise and generalize too exactly about these inner emotions. The feeling of guilt is a common one. Most people have done things of which they were ashamed. The usual procedure is to try to forget them, or blot them out with remembering that others have done these things, and worse.

What is a person to do with the feeling of guilt? The moment we have done an evil thing, the sense of that thing lingers with us. Whether it is murder, adultery, or a nasty remark, the shame of it stays with us. We try to put it from our mind, and let time wash it out. We turn to other things, and let feverish activity push it out. We may turn to drink or to drugs to give some unnatural elation to our spirits, too long depressed by these thoughts of unforgotten guilt. It may concern a quite small event. But no event with guilt attached to it is ever quite forgotten.

We run for cover, and most of us never find it. Psychology has helped us to understand that there are morbid attitudes toward past wrongs, which only add to the difficulty, because there is no hope nor help in them. But psychology cannot brush away this feeling of guilt in so light a fashion. Psychology must recognize that, in the feeling of responsibility for one's own life, lies the one possible hope of curing a person who has been escaping from life by blaming others for his or her condition. Therefore guilt holds in it, not only shame about the past, but also hope about the future. While trying to remove the

The Wonder of Forgiveness [83]

sense of guilt, psychology must be careful that it is not sawing off the only handle by which it can begin to produce the up-swing of a cure. This feeling of guilt is not only a sick feeling; it is also oftentimes a feeling of returning health, because it knows that past wrong must be faced and dealt with, not evaded and forgotten.

ON the human plane, there seem to be only two ways out of guilt. The first is to run away from it—in drugs, in pleasure, in activity, even in service or in religion. But this is like an army going through a country and destroying the buildings; if you go back, you will still find the foundations there—what was below the surface lingers. The second is to persuade yourself that what you thought was sin was not sin after all—to forgive yourself. The trouble is that this overturns the whole of moral thinking and living. We cannot exempt others as we would exempt ourselves, and therefore we know we cannot exempt ourselves. In fact, the moral principles that seem binding on us are not products of family tradition or racial taboo or religious scruple; the things are written in the universe itself, and that is why we cannot escape them. Therefore, neither of these ways really leads "out"; they lead nowhere.

Religion has always recognized this element of fear-guilt in the human heart—man's inability to deal with and expiate his own sins. The principle of animal and even human sacrifice arose out of the profoundly felt need for atonement in the human heart. We cannot bear the burden of this thing, some other must. It was never anything but a searching for something that was never found because, even in these atoning sacrifices, there was the extension of the man's desire to forgive himself. He could not really be sure of God's forgiveness, even when he felt genuinely penitent.

Then Jesus came into the world. He lived and served and taught, and men were aware that God had come to them. Finally He died on a cross. To some it looked as if this were just the price good men have often paid for achieving a great end, or going against the stream of public opinion. But the things He said Himself, and many thought about Him, notably the Apostle Paul, began to reveal the cross as God's way of dealing with the guilt and fear of unforgiveness in man. Christ had willingly taken upon Himself to bear the burden of guilt in place of man.

The cross was not man's effort to atone for his own sins; it came from the other side. It was God's offer of forgiveness. It held in it supremely and uniquely the two elements of vindication of the righteous law and of mercy toward the transgressor in which true atonement consists: no other but God Himself in Christ could so "reconcile the world unto Himself."

Ever since this realization came upon the Early Church, men have found in Jesus more than the best life that was ever lived, more than a perfect expression of the love of God; they have found in Him the Saviour, who saves man by forgiving man's sins. He is able to reach down into that dark area of confused pride, guilt, and fear, which is the inner life of so many of us, and bring about humility, forgiveness, and faith. It is nothing else than a miracle, perhaps the greatest miracle of all, and certainly the greatest doorway of hope into which men can ever enter.

Let me tell you some stories of what God's forgiveness does for people.

A sensitive and intelligent man who says he was a kind of Galahad perfectionist grew disillusioned at his own ability to achieve or create perfection, and turned to alcohol. Over a period of years he was greatly helped by Alcoholics Anonymous, but on occasions he would still go off again. There was one point of the AA program which he had not carried out, and which he realized might be causing the trouble. The fifth step in their twelve steps is, "We admit to God, to ourselves, and to another human being the exact nature of our wrongs."

He found a minister whom he felt he could trust with hearing the confession of a sin long, long gone by, which had laid unforgiven in his memory for several decades. After it had been confessed, they knelt and prayed the prayer of absolution. He rose from his knees a free man. The guilt and the shame were gone—not gone by confession, but gone by the forgiveness of God sealed through that prayer.

This story illustrates two important things: first, that the human conscience is terribly delicate, and must be met at its own highest point; and second, that oftentimes individuals need to have the forgiveness of God made real to them, not only by teaching and knowledge of the Gospel, but also by hearing the word of forgiveness spoken authentically by a minister of God.

A while ago, I was talking with a woman who had come through several months of psycho-analysis, and was making excellent progress. A very divided self —a self so divided that it was hard to tell which person you were talking to at any given time—was being brought together into one individuality in a remarkable way. I was deeply impressed with how successful this treatment was, and with its achievements to date. She happened to tell me that, before the analysis began, she had gone to a minister, made a full confession of all the past. She said to me, "At that point I let go of all my guilt, and have never returned to it."

There was in a ward of one of the state mental hospitals a woman who could not be touched nor roused from her apathy and indifference. A minister friend went to her and began talking simply to her about faith and the love of God. At first, he made no more impression than the rest, but later she called him to her and said, "The trouble with me is that I murdered my children." She told him of the circumstances, and he told her that even for this there was forgiveness from God, if she were penitent. She gave every sign that she was, and they knelt and prayed together for the forgiveness of God. He told me that, as he went out of the door of the ward, she stood by her bed, waving her hand to him with a smile on her face that no other human influence had been able to create.

How many, one wonders, in mental hospitals and outside, are sick with conscious guilt for real sins, but do not know where to turn? Medicine and psychiatry, as such, know no forgiveness. How many people feel they can trust doctors until they know they are trustworthy, with the deep and terrible secrets of their lives? Perhaps it is only to men of God, whose lips are sealed with sacred secrecy, that they can divulge these things. But certainly it is only those who believe in God, and therefore in the divine forgiveness, who can offer them any real way out. How many sick people, I wonder, would begin to get well, if once they were assured of the wonderful forgiveness of God?

Forgiveness is, I am sure, a by-product of the unfathomable love of God. He forgives, because He wants to have His children restored to fellowship with Himself. One cannot believe in the kind of God Jesus revealed without believing that God has within Him a hunger for the love of people, of which our own hunger for it is but a dim reflection. God does not need us as we need one another, for He is not finite, but it is implicit in His love that He wants us. There is law in God, and therefore judgment, but we feel this is secondary, provisional, compared with His love.

The condition of forgiveness is repentance. We cannot except nor find God's forgiveness toward what we regard lightly: we must call sin sin, if we want to be forgiven for it. We must accept our full responsibility for it, and we must try to see it as He sees it, not as our contemporary world sees it, nor as we can sometimes cajole ourselves into seeing it. I believe God does not want long brooding over our sins, nor unhealthly preoccupation with them; but a swift, honest confession of them, to be followed by the sense of His unmerited and gracious forgiveness, and this to be followed by a new start in the new life.

We know, too, that we continually stand in need of God's forgiving grace. It takes prayer and grace to keep our consciences sharp and our expectations high when we know that we fail again and again. Perhaps we are always on the way up from sin to grace, or on the way down from grace to sin, for there is no constancy in us. Yet each time when repentance and confession are real, so is the forgiveness. And therefore we get up and go on our way, miserably aware of our falls and faults, yet gloriously aware of the unbelievable goodness of God to us. There, in that double consciousness, lies the Christian secret.

Let us pray that secret down into the depths of us, and spread it wherever we can. There is more of hope and health in it than in all the plans and panaceas man ever invented. There are many ways for Christians to think of themselves, some good, some dangerous; but one need never fear to think of himself as the forgiven child of God. That will beget in him the humility and the abounding thankfulness that will keep him right before God and with men; and will fill all God's dealings with him with that most glorious of qualities, the element of joyful surprise!

9

Victory Over Self

Your Greatest Battle

W E ARE AT WAR today as surely as we were in the '40's and are in the midst of making the same mistakes again. However, the desire for victory is still in our hearts but the greed and selfishness which underlie our current war have not been touched so far.

Everyone wants to see all wars end—not outward ones only. But until we realize that the enemy is not only across the oceans, but in America, in the selfish materialism of our own hearts, in the demands we make on life and other people, in our pleasure-loving godlessness, in our want of inner control, we shall miss the real point. We must learn our lesson.

What is our lesson? I think it is that nations are no better than the men who make them up; that national policy can rise no higher than the standards of the people; that every man's greatest contribution to national life is his own faith and integrity. We have been thinking we could skip character, and live on the morals of our forefathers. Spiritual capital, like monetary, does not last forever.

We fight with force against the enemy without because we have not learned to fight with faith against the enemy within. The real war is within. What we need today, more than anything else, more even than victory in the war against aggression, are weapons, manpower, and strategy to win the war against selfishness. We need, and we must have, victory over ourselves, before any outward victory will mean anything more than temporary cessation of human conflict.

What will give us victory over ourselves? Paul gives us the source of such victory in Romans 7:25. "Thanks be to God"; and he gives us the channel of it, "through Jesus Christ our Lord." We are to seek the Christian's victory, from God and through Christ.

Let us face at the outset how many Christians are not victorious, but defeated. Defeated by circumstances, defeated by other peoples' natures and wrong-doings, defeated by the down-drag of the flesh, defeated by loss, by pain, by suffering, by worry. Instead of saying with confidence, "This is the victory that overcometh the world, even our faith," they have to say in honesty, "This is the defeat that has been caused by the world, even our self-centeredness." That is the opposite of faith. Unbelief is not the opposite of faith; self-centeredness is—being centered in self rather than in God. When I see people who pray the Lord's Prayer, who come to church, and who profess the faith, but who meet the difficulties of this life in just the same way as everybody else, with the same bitterness, the same petulant cry of "why?", the same demand of their rights, the same going down under sorrow, I know that there are many Christians in name who have never got above the lowlands of self-centered living, who have never gone up on the heights of faith, and there found victory in Christ which He is waiting to give them. But those heights are there, waiting to be climbed in faith.

There are seven victories that await those who will let God give them victory through Jesus Christ our Lord.

Victory over disposition. I don't believe there are any people with naturally good dispositions. Everyone is irritated by something in other people, or subject to moods, or impatient in getting his own way at home, or short sometimes in dealing with people. But some people lie down in that kind of defeat, wallow in it, even use it to get their own way because other people fear their reactions.

It is possible to have a good character, and a rotten disposition—to be honest and upright and be the very devil to live with. It is also possible to be very pleasant, when everything is going your way, and when your body is rested and well fed. The test comes when things are going against you, when you are tired and pressed.

I have seen Christ break a bad disposition, and give a good one in its place. The wife of a college president had a dispositional temper. She came to some meetings and went away terribly convicted. She locked herself in her room for two days—but she came out a different person. Christ had won the war for her. Think how much happier life will be for your husband or wife, for your children, for the people who wait on you in public or in private, if you will let Christ cure that grouch, that temper, that irritability, that "demandingness"! He will get at the root of the conflict which underlies it and give you His victory.

Victory over sorrow. Nothing shows the level of our faith like the way we take the sorrows which are a part of our human existence. Christianity always helps us to anticipate these things. A man dying of cancer questioned me one day why it was that his pagan friends seemed not to like to come to see him, but his Christian friends came more and more; and I ventured to say to him that I thought the reason was that Christianity faces all these things, has a place for them, knows the peace of God in the midst of them, and the assurance of the life to come.

There is not much in the "stiff upper-lip" philosophy. That breaks down before the tremendous tragedies that life holds. Our own strength is never enough. Unless you believe in the fundamental purposes of God, unless you believe in His personal care and Providence, unless you are sure that He cares and that He is working for your blessing and good, even through the seeming tragedies that happen to nearly everyone, then you must meet them in your own strength. But when you think of what Christ made of His own cross, you see that you can find victory in yours. Our victories, anyway, are only a reflection of His.

Victory over pain. Some people could get rid of pain altogether if they were not self-centered, if they did not hug the pain to them and make it a way to get attention. The victory they need is victory over self. But there is real pain in the world. Paul prayed God to take away his thorn in the flesh—whatever it was, epilepsy perhaps, or malaria—and God only said, "My grace is sufficient for thee." He did not take away the pain, or the affliction. He gave Paul the victory over it.

There are no people in the world who make me bow my head in reverence as much as those who have learned to take pain in the Christian way. They do not draw attention to it or to themselves for having it. They do not seem to fight it, but accommodate themselves to it graciously. They seem to offer it as a sacrifice to Christ, who suffered for us. What suffering must be for those who see no purpose in life and have no ultimate faith about it, I cannot imagine. But here, as everywhere else, Christ has victory for us if we will take it.

Victory over sin. This victory begins in the life and death of our Lord Himself—in His life, because He "was tempted in all points like as we are, yet without sin"—in His death, because there He took upon Himself the sin of the world, suffered in our stead, made redemption possible for us. We need to be redeemed from sin first, and to have salvation put in its place by our Saviour. Then we need to claim His power over our sins, one by one.

Most of us fight a dreary battle for character, or else give it up entirely, and just give in to the desires that assail us—desires to coddle and indulge the body, to please and amuse the mind, to fritter away the life with trivial pursuits, to win out over somebody else, to "get ours." The way to deal with sin is not to try to hate sin more, but to love Christ more. He makes the battle seem worth while. He gives us help, directly and through the church, in winning it. Studdert Kennedy used to say, "It takes a passion to conquer a passion." Now Christ is the only passion great enough to make me want to overcome my sins. There is not a sin in the catalog which He has not helped somebody to overcome.

Victory over the wrongs of others. Here many go down in defeat because they do not know Christ's philosophy of dealing with the wrongs of others. Christ refused to be bitter toward His enemies or to take their wrongs as "personal." He refused to ignore their wrongdoings, although they affected Him. He went on loving them, and He went on trying to change them. His love never stopped, and His challenge never stopped.

That is what we ought to do—not lie down and let sinful people walk away with everything—but challenge them on wrongdoing without fear or favor, and keep on loving them, believing that they can be different. Every man is compelled by the right. He is moved by it wherever we incarnate it for him, even if he hates us for it. We need to keep the courage of challenge, and the kindliness of love in our hearts, no matter what people do.

Victory over the world. Our job, as Christians, is to be in the world and not of it—to penetrate it with our own spiritual essence, and not be penetrated by it. It is hard to keep close enough to the world to touch it all the time for Christ, and yet not let it keep close enough to touch us all the time with its own "slow stain." Withdrawing, retreating Christians are no good, for they do not get near enough to the world to do anything for it. But Christians that succumb to its ways are no good, either; they are changed themselves by the very world they are supposed to change.

Yet it is possible to walk through this world, keeping close to man, yet not "going" worldly. The secret lies in a strong hold upon Christ. He did that. All mankind loves Him, yet who ever walked through this world before or since that took on none of its contamination? But we must develop the line between Him and us, so that His hold upon us is stronger than the world's.

Victory over death. "The last enemy that shall be destroyed is death," says Paul. The march of Christianity across the world was caused by the fact that the Resurrection broke like a great light above the heads of a pagan world. The gray, nameless impersonality of the pagan afterlife was superseded by a clear Christian promise of immortality. The hopeless sorrow of seeing one you love go out into the silence gave way to the assurance through faith of his continued life with God.

You may not believe this, but you must admit that it makes life far richer if you can believe it; and you must concede that the Christian belief is the strongest attestation in the world to the fact of personal immortality. Death becomes almost an incident, not something to fear but something in the natural order of things, with the great Christian promise shining through.

Dr. F. B. Meyer, one of the great Christians of another generation, wrote to a friend a day or two before his death, "I have just heard, to my surprise, that I have only a few days to live. It may be that before this reaches you

I shall have entered the Palace. Don't trouble to write. We shall meet in the morning. With much love, Yours affectionately, F. B. Meyer." That kind of faith does not come to a man in a moment, nor just by wishing. It comes as you obey and serve and trust your Lord in this life, and having found Him worthy of your trust where you can see, trusting Him where you cannot see.

ALL the victory of which we have been speaking is a derived victory. We can win the victory only because Christ won it long ago.

We participate in His victory by faith. Faith is like a wire, along which He sends the power, the love, the guidance, that enables us to share in His victory. Faith is not just a belief of the mind; faith is the set of the whole personality God-ward. It doesn't begin with beliefs but with obedience.

The first step of faith is to want to be done with the sin that stands between you and God. It may also be something that stands between you and another.

The second step of faith is to come to God whether you know Him yet or not, and surrender your sin and yourself to Him. As you do this, God will come out toward you, and you will find yourself back in the old familiar outlook of the Christian religion. It was made for people like you and me, in all stages of arrival. Christ came to "seek and save that which is lost." His church is the company of those who are trying to follow Christ and obey and serve Him.

When the knockdowns come, as they do to us all, Christians know that Christ will help them to live through whatever comes. They only wait to see what His meaning for them is, but they know that nothing happens without meaning. And when you say that, you say everything. You say that life has a solution. You say that nothing takes place in which God cannot have a share. You say that it is possible to be at all times victorious through Christ.

THE MOON THROUGH THE WINDOW

Strange moon—so bright, so shapeless in the sky,
Seen through the old glass of a windowpane
With lines and little ridges on its face,
The edges shifting, cut and shimmering,
Forming no round of silver, but a blob
Of white, like dough, against the darkening heavens.
I move my head an inch, and all lines change,
And hence the moon-shape alters once again.
Far from the usual disc, it takes the form
More of a gourd, balloon-like—or an egg—
Even as slowly the odd mass ascends
The blue of gathered evening. Every inch
Of progress makes a new, ungainly shape,
The rim is so fantastic in its change
It is as if the moon were on a drunk . . .

And yet outside, and not six feet from me,
Where any naked human eye can see,
The ancient silver circle climbs the sky
Staid and cold-sober as it ever was . . .

So may the seamy side of human things
Distort the image of the very heavens!

10.

The Secret of Fellowship

The Way to Creative Living

WE SHALL all agree that Jesus had a genius for human friendship. He was the revelation of God Himself, and the most exalted category is not sufficient to hold Him. But on the human plane He was a friendly Person who loved people, understood them, had an infinite sympathy for them, and knew supremely well how to get along with them. He seemed able to communicate something of this genius for human fellowship to His immediate friends—and of course the wonderful thing about Him is that He keeps on making immediate friends still, men and women who know Him, and learn from Him how to create and sustain the right kind of relation to people today.

So clear are the principles on which He and His people in all ages depend, that we can make a list of them. By that list we can check our own human fellowship, and from it learn to lift the level of reality in all our relationships.

THE first tenet is the principle of *concern.* "This is my commandment, that you love one another, as I have loved you." When you think of a man as a thing, you cannot think of him as a man. If you are willing just to use him for your own ends, to touch his life only as two billiard balls touch on a table to bounce away from each other unaffected, or to have no care what happens to him in fulfilling his life, then you can never have fellowship with him. Fellowship implies concern, and concern implies interest.

I believe that every life that touches ours is meant to be blessed by it. No Christian ought ever to think of a telephone operator or salesgirl or train-conductor or casual acquaintance as anything else than a "soul for whom Christ died," a person in the full sense. The mere smile of friendliness is not enough. We ought to have the concern for them which causes us to create fellowship with them up to the very limit allowed by the time and occasion.

Concern deepens with knowledge and better acquaintance, until, without attempting to play Providence, we ought to be mindful all the time of people's real development, finding the best their hearts crave, the full meeting of the demands of Christ upon their lives knowing that in meeting His demands they will find the highest possible happiness. There is plenty of room in a Christian heart for everybody. There is plenty of time for a Christian to treat everybody as a person. There is plenty of grace in God to fill our hearts with concern for every person we meet, and to draw some of those whom we meet into the glorious fellowship of all who love Christ and try to live by His grace.

THE second tenet is the principle of *candor.* We often think that what makes fellowship is a warm feeling of personal affinity; but we come to learn that this may be temporary, and may be sentimental only. What creates fellowship is self-impartation, and the impartation of ourselves means telling to others the realities about ourselves.

The other day I was with a small group of men exploring the fascinating mysteries of spiritual fellowship. One of the most reticent and intellectual of them said to us simply, "There is no substitute for letting others know about us." One watches fellowship between two people or among a group go down to a deeper, more real level, as the mere swapping of ideas turns into the passing on of something personal about ourselves. One man said he felt inferior about his own leadership, another that he knew he was wilful, another that he did not like to take the risk of doing things to which he was not accustomed. It cost them something to say these things—candor is always more costly than reserve. Later two of those men met together and were candid not only about their own, but about each other's needs.

Truth is the tonic of fellowship. It keeps it from becoming soft and squashy. We all have a general idea that fellowship is wonderful and we want it very much, but sometimes we are not willing to pay the cost of it. The cost is chiefly the willingness to go through the pain of giving and receiving the corrective of the truth. We put ourselves out of fellowship in two ways—by refusing to be honest with others when we see them doing a wrong thing, or a right thing in the wrong way; or by refusing to receive from them the same tonic honesty as to our own needs. We can be pretty sure that when someone is a good enough friend to say something candidly but lovingly critical of us to our faces, the truth is probably more, rather than less, than what they say. Mere brutal frankness is only cruelty, but "speaking the truth in love" is an apostolic command, and it is much more—it is the only way of renewal and progress in human relations. No home is secure, no relationship is sound, without the element of loving candor.

This must work both ways. If we give it, but will not take it, we are dominating. If we take it, but will not give it, we are doormats. We become whole people under God when we deal in the truth spoken in love, receiving it from others even if it hurts, and giving it to them even if it costs us to do it. Do not hold secret criticisms of people; they fester and grow. "If we walk in the light, as he is in the light, we have fellowship one with another." Walking in the light is not the moonshine of affected spirituality. Walking in the light is dealing ever in the truth, living by it, seeking it, welcoming it, knowing that in the end only "the truth shall make you free."

THE third tenet of fellowship is the principle of the cell. Every person who is interested in learning what Christian fellowship really is needs to be one of a little Christian company. John Wesley filled England with little companies of twelve. They had a leader, and they met once a week. They were honest about where they were living spiritually, and helped to hold each other up to Christian standards. Lecky says John Wesley saved England from revolution. Do you see any connection between these small nuclei of people bound closely together in spiritual cells, lifting the level of the moral and spiritual life of the people who belonged to them, and so lifting the moral and spiritual level of the nation and keeping a nation from going the way France went in that same century— France which did not have a John Wesley, or a spiritual revival?

Personally I think that there is nothing which is so much needed in America today as the multiplication of small groups of people who meet regularly to pray, to talk, to help one another, and to plan. Most people attempt to be Christians in isolation, that is—in a vacuum. They come to church, but they remain profoundly isolated, spiritually, from everyone else. I am more and more convinced that Christian character is of no significance apart from Christian relationships. You cannot be a Christian man or woman just in yourself, but only as your faith works out into transformed relationships.

We have not saved the world by saving individuals because we have sought Christian character rather than Christian relationships; we have tried to build faith into individual souls without realizing that it is of the essence of Christian life that it issue and find its fulness in Christian community. Few of us can live in regularly constituted Christian "communities" (in the technical sense, like monasteries, etc.), though our homes ought all to be miniature Christian communities, but we can all be part of a spiritual cell which is our first step out of our spiritual loneliness and individualism, and in which we find the chief factors of Christian community.

Such groups are springing up in many places and in many ways today. One friend of mine has started weekly breakfast gatherings in fifty-six cities. Two of them, I happen to know, are in very strategic places for the good of this nation. I do not hesitate to say that I believe the first step away from spiritual babyhood and irresponsibility and ineffectiveness for most people is in the direction of becoming a part of such cells, perhaps setting one of them in motion. If you want to start an awakening in America, you must be awakened yourself. And I believe God may awaken America through awakening small groups together, who may learn the way of Christ in companies.

THE fourth tenet of fellowship is the principle of a *common cause.* We cannot seek fellowship as an end in itself, for we shall not find it. Even if we find it for a time, it will wither later. For fellowship, as the individual Christian character, is not in itself enough. Jesus loved the people about Him, and they loved Him and each other, but they did not follow Him because it was pleasant to have such close friends. They followed Him because He had always in His eye the great cause of the Kingdom. Fellowship would be too personal, too personality-centered —let us say it frankly—too selfish, if it did not constantly look away from its own self-conscious life to the healing of the sickness of the world. Fellowship, like character, must exist for something. It is not two dots at the ends of a line; it is a triangle with three points, and the third point is some one portion of the Kingdom's business which we agree to carry out together.

Friends are good. Christian friends are better. But Christian people whose congeniality issues forth in concern for a worthwhile commitment is best of all. When we match wits, thrash out policies, fight through up-hill times, rejoice in conquests together, then we have found the pitch and zenith of Christian fellowship. In this sense, fellowship can hardly be self-consciously pursued; it is rather a by-product of selfless action toward accepted ends.

I have seen small groups start and fail—and why? Because they sought fellowship for itself, or for their own satisfaction. Our joy in them is incidental, secondary, though very real. Even what they do for us spiritually is of minor importance, compared to what they do together for the kingdom of God throughout the world. We need to look often across into one another's eyes, with love, with truth and with trust, but then we both need to look away from ourselves to the huge task that confronts all Christians today, and vow to one another the loyalty that it will take to storm and conquer and hold one outpost in the front line of the Kingdom.

THE fifth tenet of fellowship is the principle of a Christ-centered life. In the absolute sense, this is the most important principle of all. For a great common loyalty is more important even than a great common cause. One can be humanly associated with others in great enterprises and derive much pleasure and benefit from that association, but there is something infinitely more profound in really meeting in Christ. When our human selves are bound together within the bracket which points upward to Him, they have a deeper bond than any other in the world. It is at once more personal and less personal, it is committed to the great cause, yet free of self-effort, for He inspires what is done—it is constantly renewed and refreshed by His over-arching presence.

We may say that true Christian fellowship is not triangular, but pyramidal. It does not consist of you and me and the Cause—it consists of you and me and the Cause at the base, and Christ at the apex. He is the missing factor in so much human association. What shall keep these strutting egos of ours from making us want to dominate even a fellowship ourselves? What shall bring harmony when disharmony arises, as it always will at some time in human associations? What shall keep us continually under the consciousness that our wisdom is so little and our pride so great that we must ever remember our weaknesses and shortcomings, even while we stand by the truth as we see and understand it? In the end we are all children and need an Authority.

Some of us fear human authority. We have always feared it, and we have cause to fear it today more than we ever did before. When men are given power over men it is fatal for both. Yet we *need* a power over us. And we find it in the gracious Christ Himself, as He moderates our divergences and mitigates our disputes and comes with the last word, as we wait upon Him in common humility and faith. He is the real Leader of every Christian fellowship, and must have not only the recognition which causes us to give assent to the statement, but actual regency which causes us to wait freshly upon Him again and again. The relationships, the fellowship, which He is allowed to guide, to which He is ever the great Third Party, are the surest pledge to ourselves that we are really His men and women; and they are, I believe, the most potent Christian leaven for human society which we can possibly find.

I want such thoughts as these to be a growing-point, a point of departure for experimentation. The reason why many people calling themselves Christians never become vital and effectual and contagious is not because they do not believe the right things theologically, or have not enough faith. It is because they have never ventured into the realm of realistic Christian fellowship. They may be friendly and even unselfish people, but they are walled away in a prison of self-consciousness, of self-centeredness, which is self-made, and from which the only exit is in self-giving.

A fine scholar of our church said recently, "We avoid deep religious fellowship to avoid talking about the deepest things. Formal religion is an escape from the problems of our own living. This is due to fear. Our church lacks a reality of Christian life. Only in the openness of Christian fellowship can anything happen. We have got to talk about what we have experienced."

Our want is not primarily intellectual, though we need more truth; it is not primarily moral, though our very isolation tends to create defeat within us. Our want is a want of living Christian relationships which total up in Christian fellowship. The only church that can save the world is a church that has learned how to touch the world's unreconciled in spiritual fellowship under the mighty hand of Christ. To create such an atmosphere and to make it available to all is the church's greatest task and next step.

11.

Communicating Your Faith

How You Can Help Other People

IF WE KNOW ANYTHING about the Christian religion, we know that from the beginning it has spread largely by the contagion of the faith of its adherents. And if we know anything about our contemporary world, we know that a great surge of faith would probably do more for us than anything that could possibly happen. We also know that people, who were not open to it a few years ago, today are astonishingly open to faith rightly presented.

Christians seem divided into two classes: (1) the emotional, half-baked and immature, who after they find faith go off in all directions, pressing it unwisely upon other people; and (2) the shy and self-conscious people, terribly aware of both the magnitude of the task and of their own unworthiness, who give up before they start.

There is a story pertaining to the latter about an Irish professor who was once asked, "Are you saved?" And he replied, "To tell you the truth, my good fellow, I am, but it was such a narrow squeak it doesn't bear talking about."

How far from the bumptiousness of the first group, and the funk of the second, is Jesus' simple confident call to Peter and Andrew at their nets, "Follow me and I will make you to become fishers of men!"

We know what an unlikely lot of men they were to whom these words were spoken. Few of them were educated. It is dubious how many had ever been a hundred miles from where they were, or even fifty. It would have terrified them if anyone had told them that the fate of the Christian cause, and indeed of the world it was meant to save, hung largely on what they did. Yet Jesus believed that they could and would become fishers of men. They did.

We are Christians today because they did, and others like them who came after them. He goes on laying down that same call before all who become His disciples, "Follow me and I will make you to become fishers of men."

LET us explore some ways by which we may do this kind of work effectively.

To make faith real to others, it must first be real to us. We cannot give away anything we do not have. None of us has everything Christianity has to give us, and we must be growing in the new life all the time. We do not need to be great saints to do this work, else none would ever do it but a handful in every age. But we *do* need to be genuine believers who have made an honest beginning in Christian discipleship.

Faith must be less of an aspiration and more of a force. We must try to live with our hand in God's, being led by Him, not trying to lead Him into doing what we want. Saintliness we may not have, but single-minded commitment we can and must have.

Then we must witness to our faith. We all know that technically a witness is someone who is present when something of significance happens. When he speaks of an automobile accident he saw or a man running from a house he robbed, he speaks firsthand. A witness is not only someone who has seen something but someone who tells others what he has seen. It would hardly occur to a man brought into court to testify as to what he had seen that it would be enough if he merely "behaved" as if he had seen it; the court wants his word on it.

A proclamation of faith does two things: (1) it greatly fortifies the person who makes it and puts steel into his own decision; and (2) it greatly moves the ordinary hearer of it, for living faith is one of the most contagious things in the world.

You can see that one of the convincing and moving things about such a witness is the freshness and contemporary quality of it. You do not announce a faith you have held thirty years quite as you do one you found last week. Yet a faith thirty years old ought to be much better and stronger than one that began last week.

How can we keep our faith fresh and up to date? Only by steadily growing, by new and present discoveries in it, by being always in a continuing crucible of experience. When religion is merely habit its contagion disappears, but when religion is daily experience, in which you and I are not way over in mature sainthood, but struggling still with ourselves and our sins, yet knowing some victories too, people will listen to us.

The old boy who used to get up in Wednesday night prayer meetings and say the same thing he had said for years won few people and lost many. On the other hand, the timid girl or man just beginning who said less and said it with misgiving and hesitation, yet said it nevertheless, touched everyone. The old boy knew more theology, maybe, and said it more correctly, but the new person brought to it freshness and humility—the humility that stems, not from lack of conviction, but from knowing that one has not progressed very far.

The people who are fond of telling you that they have "always belonged to the Church" are apt to sound proud in saying it, and they lose contact with those who do not share their estimable habit of going to church. But if we are ourselves in the crucible of experience, failing yet finding fresh victory, always learning yet ever stronger in faith, then we can make this real to other people.

Talk about events and about people, not about ideas and convictions only. The original Gospel was "good news." If the early Christians reached for something to say to a pagan or unbeliever in their time, they would say something about a person or an event, often about a supreme event in the life of a supreme Person such as His Resurrection.

Where religion is alive, it creates a stir and sets people to talking. Sometimes their talk is negative and critical, and we must learn how much of this arises, not from objective and valid question, but from stung consciences, from the fact that this new person or situation has convicted them deeply of their immaturity and ineffectiveness and need of genuine surrender to God. But when people are interested enough to criticize, they may be also interested enough to hear the other side.

We must not argue, though we should be able to give good account of our faith. We shall win by witness, by simple telling of what has happened to us and to other people. The Acts of the Apostles is one long buzz and stir of opposition and acceptance concerning Christ and His Gospel. How has the church ever settled down in such a routine manner that it causes neither great criticism nor great enthusiasm?

We are all likely to talk about people. Why not turn your gossip into something constructive? Don't talk about what an awful thing Mrs. Jones did, but talk about the change that has come into Mrs. Smith's life since she made a Christian decision and put her problems in God's hands. Don't talk about what a crooked deal old Brown pulled in his business, but talk about the way Williams has changed since he began praying about his business and getting some of his friends together to do the same thing. There is plenty that is positive, if you will learn it.

Now everybody has a problem, or lives near one. A battle with drugs, or a difficult in-law, or someone desperately ill, or a feeling of futility about life in general, or a hard decision to make—everybody faces these things at times. A noted minister friend has said that a man is like an island, sometimes you have to row all around him before you find a place to land. Rowing around him means friendship, thoughtfulness of him, seeing him when you can in natural ways, and praying for him.

Don't accuse people, and if possible don't say to them what it is much better they say to you. You may know it all along, but keep quiet and remember the advantage of their saying what the problem is. Most people want to talk about themselves and will do so if you give them a sympathetic chance. Be a good listener. Don't pitch in too soon with your answer; get the problem into the open, with sympathy and no taking sides or attitudes.

Someone sent a friend to see me recently and told me on the phone how bad a life he was living. He ended, "Give him the devil."

I said, "But he's already *got* the devil—what I want to give him is God! The devil has been causing him to do the things he's done, and he's been in hell. It's not my business to give him the devil; it's my business to put him next to Somebody who can take the devil out of him!"

Let us keep to the great spiritual laws, but not work off spleen or "righteous indignation" or puritanical pharisaism on anybody. The Christian religion is for sinners only— no one else. You and I can only help others as we know we are sinners—forgiven ones, but continuing ones just the same.

For many people, especially in the depths of difficulty, religious faith is a distant dream. They face grim, un-welcome realities—what has faith got to do with them? Our job is to help them turn aspiration into experiment. Of course they like faith. How do they find it? They find it when they hand over their situation and themselves, into God's hands. They say something like this, "Lord, I am not doing very well with this. I want to give it to You, and to find Your solution to it. I take my hands off that You may put Yours on."

In the quiet of such surrender miracles often begin to happen. Anxiety goes, and tension; fear goes, and rebellion. We do not ask God to do what we want; we ask Him to do what He wants. We pray and keep praying. We rise from a prayer like that different ourselves, and therefore different in our attitude toward the difficulty. Our fears fix the situation so that nothing can happen; faith unsticks it, liquefies it, gives God a chance to work in it.

Remember, too, that the greatest news of all is that real faith is real adventure. There was a fine sentence in the Simon Stylites Column of the *Christian Century* once which said: "It is an axiom, to me at least, that the amount of good a person can do depends greatly on how much fun he gets out of it."

You know how many people there are for whom religion is a prohibition. It warns us against fun. It is almost a price we pay for our fun. Have you ever discovered that the greatest of all fun is in trying to live out the will of God? There usually is a cross in that somewhere, but I believe Jesus was a deeply happy Person, and wants us to be.

Take off that solemn look, and get a spiritual twinkle in your eye, if you want to beat sin at its own game of giving people fun! We have got the greatest adventure in the world. We want them to share in it.

Some of you think of this as salesmen do, and I wish more people used their ordinary secular brains for God. Let me give you *seven steps* that may help you in making faith real to others.

Prospect. This is the person you want to reach. Pray to be shown who he is. It may be an old friend, or a sudden chance contact—a social friend, or a business acquaintance. Learn all you can about him. Make real friends with him.

Problem. As you talk, people talk about themselves. You must get on their side, on the side of their best selves. You are interested in them as people, not just as prospects, even for faith. They reveal themselves when they trust you.

Product. You must know your Lord and your faith, and know what faith is doing in typical modern lives and situations. Women aren't interested in all the mechanics of a dishwasher, but they want to watch it wash dishes. Events should be the climate, not arguments—samples, not sales talk.

Proposition. Begin talking of how faith will help individuals in their actual situations. It can only happen if they let it happen—if they turn aspiration into experiment. Somewhere talk must stop and the trial of prayer and faith begin. Tell them how it begins with self-surrender and "let go-and-let-God."

Promise. Tell others of Christ's great promise: "Behold, I stand at the door and knock: if any man will open unto me, I will come in. . . ." Then there is the other promise, our promise to give ourselves to Him in faith and dedication. That needs to be sealed, not only by verbal resolution, but by prayer and promise to God Himself.

Procedure. Give an individual something to go on with —help with daily prayers and Scripture, and with going to church. Get him, if possible, into a training group where he will learn and articulate and apply.

Program. A person is a field one day, and should be a force the next. God needs people to build the Kingdom. Faith ought to make homes and businesses different.

We ought to take on, if not the whole of the Kingdom, then specifically one of its segments we can work in. We are in God's life and work the rest of our days, living differently, praying differently, letting God through.

But remember—we do not do it. He does it. "Follow me and I will make you to become fishers of men."

12.

Dealing With Other People's Sins

What Everyone Should Know

WHAT SHALL we do about other people's sins? If we could get the right answer to that question, I think we could lessen the amount of fresh evil that we all contribute to the world's unhappy life by just about ninety-five per cent.

We meet other people's sins all day long, and the effects of them. Many of life's crises and much of its long-standing misery come from the wrongs that other people do. We are never free from these things as caused by others, and they are never free from them as caused by us. They constitute evil enough without our adding to the evil by taking them in the wrong way.

Sometimes these wrongs touch us directly. A business partner turns out to be sly and dishonest and involves us in his own dishonesties. Another woman comes into the picture and takes a man away from his lawful wife. Some-one is left in charge of an estate in which we have an interest, plays fast and loose with its investments, and we lose by it. One could add endlessly to the list. A minister comes in contact with dozens of these wrongs almost every week of his life.

Or these sins of other people may touch those whom we love or for whom we feel responsible. We know a dependent woman with a rascally brother who gets away with the money he was supposed to be taking care of in her behalf. A woman walks out on her husband and children; they are neighbors of ours and we carry a concern for them.

Someone makes what we think a bad mistake in relation to our children—a teacher planting atheistic or subversive ideas in their minds, a playmate getting them into some kind of scrape, even a Scout leader or church school teacher taking a line with them which we feel to be mistaken. We are not directly hurt ourselves, but we smart and burn vicariously for wrongs done to other people for whom we feel pity or concern or responsibility.

What attitude should we take? What course should we pursue?

LET us think first about some of the attitudes we often do take and the course we begin to pursue, perhaps before we have had time to think.

We are likely to feel first a flash of indignation. We may "hit the roof," as the expression is. We have a ready epithet for people who do as this person has done, and we fit it quickly to him. "That so-and-so, and he sitting up in church on Sunday and singing hymns as if he wasn't a rotten hypocrite from head to foot. . . ." If a passing thought comes into our minds that we are not perfect ourselves, we comfort ourselves by saying, "I may not be too good, but at least I don't do that," which puts the other fellow way down and us quite a ways above him.

If someone else breaks in on our moral tirade, we may drop the matter from speech, but go on chewing our cud about it in silence. Or we may come back to it again, saying, "But this is righteous indignation. This really was an awful thing that he did. We must uphold what is right. . . ." All of which has some truth and justification in it, but not very much light on how we should meet wrongs done by others.

Then we begin to tell about the wrong. We do not go to the person involved, we go to others who will shake their heads morally with us and exclaim, "Too bad," when they rather enjoy hearing of it.

It gives us a feeling of moral superiority to be condemning someone else. We seem to gain something in stature by putting somebody else down. We want comfort in the sin of condemnation, so we feel people out a little before going into the whole story; and when we feel free to tell it, we bring it all out.

With the telling, it gets worse. By now there are two more sinners adding to the sin of the first one!

Now the truth is that nothing is ever gained, and much is often lost, by going to a third person with a tale. It is a sure way of making a bad matter worse. It adds to the weight of sin that the person condemned is already carrying, the added load of still more condemnation. It sets loose in the air negative and unkind emotions. If the third party is no more responsibile in handling other people's sins than you are, all this just gets multiplied and spread abroad.

It would be a great and good thing if all who call themselves Christians, and all who work and worship in the church, would seal their own mouths forever from speaking to a third person about anybody's sins. We should save almost all church rows. We should save an immense amount of time spent by ministers and others in trying to heal breaches between people. We should keep our own lives free from one of the most pharisaical and hypocritical of sins, the telling abroad of other people's sins.

There are, it seems to me, three attitudes we can take toward other people's sins. We can abjure; we can endure; or we can cure, or at least try to.

WHEN we abjure, we renounce the person. We do not wish to see him. We "keep out of his way," as we say. Some things, we tell ourselves, are not so bad, but this is really too much. We simply cannot be seen with such a person.

I think there is as much guilt and wickedness as you can find anywhere in the kind of church member who withdraws from an alcoholic, especially an unconfessed and unadmitted alcoholic, who if the church member really had any humility and faith he ought to be willing to try to help. His withdrawal and detachment of himself from great human need does not point to his own superior goodness; it points to his pride, his Pharisaism, his spiritual powerlessness. Far better, I believe, in God's sight the fellow-drunk who goes to him with what kindness he can take, than the so-called Christian who wraps his skirts about himself and will not be tarnished by the sins of one who now becomes to him an outcast.

When a person has done something to us that we think beyond forgiveness, we no longer make any attempt to repair the relation. We say we forget it—forget him. We sometimes say that such a person is to us as one dead. There are people in many churches who have said that about members of their own family. The trouble is we cannot and do not forget. The memory of that broken relation, and our part in keeping it broken, lies festering in our minds. We think of it persistently, never so much as when we determine not to. When, to the wrong another has done us, we add the wrong of lovelessness and unforgivingness, we compound the sin. We must never forget the wise and profound saying, "It is harder to forgive those whom we have wronged than those who have wronged us." We cannot put people out of our minds. We cannot even do it when they are dead. Nothing puts the wrong out of our minds but righting it.

SOMETIMES we decide just to endure. There is a husband with a vile temper. The wife did not see it when they were engaged for he kept it under, but as soon as they were married it began to show itself. She long ago decided to put up with it, and she is still putting up with it. That is no answer. If he has it at home, he has it elsewhere. It curses other people beside his family.

Mere enduring is no answer. I knew an imperious, rich woman, married to rather a gentle, almost saintly man. Her father told him when they were married that she was "a spirited girl, and you had better give her her head." They were married for more than fifty years. He put up with worldliness and materialism that might have been cured if early in their life he had taken with her the line he should have taken. Lots of times we "endure," not from any considered thought, but just because we don't want to make matters worse and we don't know what to do. Mere enduring is no answer.

What if we decide we'd like to try at least to help *cure* the sin of another? Let me make a few suggestions:

First, let us always go to sinners as a sinner ourselves. Nobody in this world is in any position to condemn nor preach to others as if he stood somewhere above them. All of us in the Christian fellowship are sinners, forgiven sinners, but sinners first, last, and all the time.

It is Christ who is righteous, not we. It is He and His righteousness, not we or ours, that we try to hold up. A person honestly trying to follow Him has something to say to one who is not, and he should say it, but with plenty of humility, knowing his own weakness. God can only use this, never our pretenses.

Second, let us pray for the person. We shall find that we cannot pray for him until we forgive him. If we try to pray when we feel proud and condemnatory, we simply will find ourselves unable to do it. It is impossible to pray to God about the sins of others till we have been honest about our own sins. This causes us to stand, not above the person for whom we pray but *beside* him, where we belong —especially in the presence of God. Prayer may do very much to loosen up our own constricted and unyielding attitudes, and may do the same for him.

Third, if it seems right, and when it seems right, let us go to him to try to talk things out. If there has been any wrong on our side, even in the way we have taken his wrongdoing, it may be well to begin with that; otherwise, we may seem to be coming in a spirit of condemnation.

We are not universally successful, but we are often successful, if we begin this way. It encourages the other person to be honest instead of defensive about his own wrongs. Our personal humility as against pride and self-righteousness, our humor and good nature when he expects a scolding, our awareness of our faults as well as his, all these will tend to get things opened up on the right basis.

Fourth, let us then speak plainly about what has happened. If we are wrong about what we think are facts, let us be open to correction on them; yet we know and he knows that wrong has been done. Let us not fear to put the right name to it, and to challenge him about it. It is terribly important that we keep the attitude of humility and the spirit of prayer all the way through. It is also important not to mince matters.

"The truth shall make you free." That means we must learn the truth, face the truth, and admit the truth—then it will make us free. Our tone of voice is important, as well as keeping self-justification out of it, and anything like recrimination. Bathed in prayer, and in a desire not to get even but to restore the relationship, frank speaking, "speaking the truth in love" as Paul calls it, can work wonders.

This course is not universally guaranteed to succeed, however, and there are times when an impartial, wise, and spiritually-minded third party may have to be called into the picture. Listen to these very concrete commands from our Lord Himself: "If your brother sins against you, go and tell him his fault, between you and him alone. If he listens to you, you have gained your brother. But if he does not listen, take one or two others along with you, that every word may be confirmed by the evidence of two or three witnesses. If he refuses to listen to them, tell it to the church; and if he refuses to listen even to the church, let him be to you as a Gentile and a tax-collector." There is complete moral realism, and also a court of last resort. I would remind you that "telling it to the church" would not mean spreading it abroad by gossip, but bringing it before a responsible company who would act like a jury in helping to find the truth and the justice of the situation.

If none of this works, we rest the case. We cast bitterness out of our hearts. We wait for the minor healing processes of time, and the major healing processes of prayer, to do their work. We bow to the imperfect human situation, and to the fact that we are not God with the whole answer in our hands.

But we do not consign the wrongdoer to limbo. We go on hoping and we go on praying. No Christian ever puts anybody else in a finally hopeless category. That, I think, is part of what Christ meant when He said, "Judge not. . . ." Do not put people in fixed and final categories, where you look upon them without hope.

There is the remaining matter of forgiveness. Our Lord spoke about few things so often. After He had given the Lord's Prayer, He went back to one petition of it, and said, "For if ye forgive not men their trespasses, neither will your heavenly Father forgive you your trespasses." That does not mean petulance on God's part, but God's recognition of His own law.

You and I will suffer for our withheld forgiveness. It will hurt us; it is bound to. Strictly speaking, we can only forgive one who recognizes that he has done us a wrong, and seeks to make it right, and asks us for forgiveness. But you and I can prevent this from happening by our censoriousness, our general and gossipy criticism, our proud and self-righteous disdain toward him. It may be that before such a person can ask for forgiveness, he may need to feel in us forgivingness, readiness to forgive.

When a wrong has been done, it takes two to right it—the one who committed it and the one against whom it was committed. The spirit of hope for reconciliation, prayer that it may take place, the removal of all obstacles on our side—that is what constitutes "forgivingness." And a Christian must always strive to maintain it.

The truth is, no other human being is beyond redemption, and you and I in our way may stand right now, in just as much need of it as someone who has done a clear and obvious wrong. Mindful of the indissoluble connection between God's forgiveness of us, and our forgiveness of one another, let us keep in mind what our Lord said:

"Whenever you stand praying, forgive, if you have anything against any one, so that your Father also who is in heaven may forgive you your trespasses."

And also what Paul said, "Let all bitterness and wrath and anger and clamor and slander be put away from you, with all malice, and be kind to one another, tender-hearted, forgiving one another, as God in Christ forgave you."

13

Four Steps to the New Life

How to Get Going and Keep Going

A S ONE follows the mind of Jesus through reading the gospels, two things become perfectly clear. The first is that all His early followers were only accepting His own verdict of Himself when they thought of Him as God come in the flesh, and as having within Himself all that man needs to understand the meaning of his life and to live it as it should be lived. Jesus thought of Himself as literally "the way, the truth and the life."

The second is that, set down in that relatively obscure and small country, subjugated to the Roman yoke, He was convinced that what He came to bring was intended for all men, and must be carried to them. With a sublime indifference to hindrances of communication, and the limitations of His first believers, He calmly told them to go and preach His Gospel to every creature.

Nearly any Christian who is even a little touched with

the spirit of Christ will agree that His message should be brought to the world. The question is, how?

The bringing of His message to the world is usually called "evangelism." The word comes from two Greek words which mean "well" and "message." The "well message" is the "good news"; and the spreading of it is called by its own name, evangelism. Push aside any unfortunate connotations the word may have for you, and go right back to the beginning. Stand before Jesus as He tells His people to go into all the world, and give the "good news" to all people.

What is the means by which this is done? I believe that, beneath all differences, there are four sides to an effective evangelism, which are always present when Christian evangelism is present, and which constitute ways and means that are open to all, whereby we can do our part in carrying out His great command. These four sides may be called the "quadrilateral of evangelism."

THE first side is *conversion*. We do not transmit alone an objective Gospel, a set of doctrines or facts that we have received in a block. We transmit the truth as it is in Christ mixed with our own experience. The blind man, in John 9, was only growingly clear as to who Jesus was, but he was very clear that, before he came to Jesus he was blind, and after he came to Jesus he could see.

The Christian faith does not become effective in the world until that faith is mixed with personal experience. We must be part of the truth we transmit, and we must let it be a part of us. It comes to others through the crucible of life. That is why we must be converted before we can evangelize. It is impossible to hand the Gospel on, as if you would take a wrapped package delivered to you, and deliver it to someone else unopened. Lots of Christians are like that; they seek to hand it on without ever finding out really what it is like.

Let us ask two questions: What are we converted from? And whom are we converted to?

We are converted from the whole of that state which is described in the New Testament by the word "sin." And it means everything from obvious "sins," like anger and pride and lust and laziness, right on up and out to living in the world as if there were no God. The state of sin is really the state of being away from God. You do not have to be doing evil to be in a state of sin; you only have to be away from God, out of Christ, separated from the faith that was meant to save you.

Christianity looks upon the vast amount of human character and goodness and generosity that know nothing of God with only mixed approval, because the chief thing in this world is not human goodness, but God. The chief element in the "good life" is not character, but faith —not human kindness, but the help of God. So we are converted, not only from the grip of our "sins," and not only from that thralldom to self and time and this world which is the essence of paganism, but from all efforts to be good "on our own."

To whom are we converted? Not to a set of vague ideals. Not to a humanly conceived "good life." Not to our own "better selves." We are converted, as Christians, to Jesus. Therefore we must know who Jesus is. We can begin with a simple view of Him as a good man.

But we shall soon find Him performing acts, making statements and claims, that put Him in a far different category from that of a mere "good man," though He was a good man. He was not always "meek and mild." Sometimes He was quite terrible, and left no doubt that He considered Himself the spiritual Master and Lord of men and of the world. He left no doubt that He believed Himself the Incarnate Son of God.

All kinds of liberal thinking from that day to this have attempted to water this down, in the interests of a more palatable faith. The point is not what is palatable for modern minds. The point is what is true. It is the consensus of the deepest and most universal thinking about Him that He was and is precisely what He said—Incarnate God. That is the apostolic and the Nicene and the universal belief about Him. You must yourself believe it before you know how inescapably true it is.

We become converted to Him when we accept Him in all His regal claims, saying often on our way perhaps, "Lord, I believe; help thou mine unbelief," but coming back to Him again and again, each time with more conviction about who He is. We are converted when we make an act of faith which accepts Him on His own terms, and surrender ourselves to Him, abandoning our sins so far as we can, and letting His life pour into us and through us.

THE second side of the quadrilateral of evangelism is *prayer*. Prayer is both the new dimension and the new language of the new life. Prayer is a different avenue to power. Our age is power-conscious, but many have yet to discover that this is the most powerful power of all. We can pray from any depth of need, from any hell-hole of sin, from any distance of skepticism and unbelief whatever. A cry to God in the darkness is heard by Him in the light. We all do pray at times. Only we must grow in prayer.

Many of us have discovered that true prayer begins where we can begin to say with Jesus, "Not my will, but thine be done." That should not mean mere resignation to fate; it should mean cooperation with the will of God.

If it helps God to get His will done for us to cry out in earnest petition for what we rightly desire, let us do it with our whole heart. I believe that often it does. Hence prayer is not just passive yielding, it is active obedience and cooperation. It is active love for God in action. It is the highest form of love for people.

We should all have regular established times for prayer, for example, in the early morning and at the end of the day. We should try various ways of praying, with the help of written prayers and of books on prayer that will guide our minds. But then let the soul take its own flight and use its own words, and become more and more child-like and simple the closer it gets to God, till our spirits are merged with His Spirit in genuine communion.

We also badly need groups for prayer. Jesus knew and spoke about the added power that comes when several are praying together. It is a most glorious experience of spiritual power, and of fellowship together. It seems to call down greater answers, greater help from God; and if He has ordained it so, this is the case. Some of us are shy about this and must get over it. Some children are shy about coming into a room full of people; you must help them get over it. It is normal for real Christians to gather and pray together, sub-normal for them not to do so. For prayer is both the continuance of our conversion to Jesus and the strength by which we carry on the gracious work of evangelism.

THE third step in the quadrilateral of evangelism is *fellowship*. Jesus did not drop the seeds of the Gospel into a dozen individual hearts. He drew a dozen men about Him and kept them with Him till they grasped who He was and what He wanted to do in the world. When you came to Him, you didn't just come to Him, you came also to His followers, His church, His Body. There is no trace nor foundation anywhere in the New Testament of that odd modern notion that a person can seek Jesus alone in a book, or by a prayer, and alone walk with Him and carry out His principles into living.

Historic Christianity knows no such thing. It is usually a selfish and abortive thing. He gave His life and His cause to His church. When you become His, you become ours, too; and when He becomes yours, we become yours, also. The inward thing is conversion. The outward thing is baptism. The inward sustenance is prayer. The outward sustenance is Holy Communion, which you can only enjoy in the fellowship of the church. The church is not always what it should be, because it is more like a school or hospital than it is like a museum; and because there are so many people in it who are too much like you and me and get complacent and stop growing. But, with all its human admixtures and failure, it is still His fellowship and it must therefore be ours.

But the fellowship of Christ is not just the outward

temple of God's House, nor just the Body of Christ, it is also the fellowship of the Holy Spirit. Because we are very finite and fallible, and understand a little at a time, the small company of believers and seekers is often the most potent of all fellowship companies.

In one of our universities where I was preaching, I spent the afternoon with about twenty undergraduates. God was in that place. One man's life was vitally changed. I saw him later and his spiritual growth is remarkable. Five or six groups have sprung up out of that gathering and now meet regularly. Seek such a company. Form one. Pray to be led to someone with whom you can begin a prayer-fellowship. It may lead you into a realm of power and spiritual joy and effectiveness which you have never known before. And many persons who can be touched no other way when brought into such companies become aware that "God is among you" and find Him in and through the fellowship.

THE fourth side of the quadrilateral of evangelism is *witness*. Jesus told us to confess Him before men. We confess Him aright by life and by word. Our lives ought to speak louder than our words. But as a matter of fact they do not, and perhaps cannot. For while our example may be potent, when we face trouble courageously, or live an evidently disciplined and unselfish life, no mere life can give testimony to all the richness of the Christian Gospel.

I cannot, by being good, tell men of Jesus' atoning death and Resurrection, nor of my faith in His divinity. The emphasis is too much on me, and too little on Him. Our lives must be made as consistent as we can make them with our faith, but our faith, if we are Christians, is vastly greater than our lives. That is why the "word" of witness is so important. And that is why it is so important that the simplest of Christians know their faith, know some theology, and can give witness to what they believe about Jesus.

Often this begins in something He has done for us. When you meet persons suffering from the tensions that are so rife today, and can tell them that He gives you release in your heart and your body, it makes them recognize power in Him. We must often seek to come to the place of their need, so that our witness is relevant witness, not irrelevant. We do not need to wait till we are great saints to do this, and if we wait we shall never do it. Begin where you are, with what you believe and with those you know.

Don't go pious or professional, be perfectly natural and simple, but be unafraid either of people or of giving voice to what you believe about Christ. Do not say you cannot do this kind of thing. You may not be able to do it just as somebody else does it, but you can do it as God leads you.

What is a church full of tongue-tied people in a world full of vocal materialists? It is a cipher! But what might happen if all of us began praying to God for a more courageous and effective witness—so that wherever we go there is the obvious joy, the adventure, the clear faith, of Christians—so that, humbly and when the occasion is right, we speak up about our faith!

And so these four sides of evangelism remain—conversion, prayer, fellowship, and witness. And there is no "greatest of them," for they stand together like the four walls of a strong building. Let them become the solid walls of your life, of your church. And we shall see the modern, grassroots, everyman-edition of Jesus' last and greatest command, "Go ye into all the world, and preach the Gospel to every creature."

To an Organist

"Through Jesus Christ our Lord"
You wait for that—
And when those words are said
Your hands obedient fall upon the keys
And strike—for us to sing thereby—
"Amen" . . .

"Through Jesus Christ our Lord."
Would God our hands not only
But our heart and head
Obedient answered, when those words were said:
And every inmost hope, each thought, each word
Echoed "Through Jesus Christ our Lord"—
And when those words were uttered, then
We answered with our life,
"Amen!"

14.

Spiritual Power

The Force Which Makes Life Different

WE BELIEVE, as Christians, that Jesus was the manifestation of God in human life, that, as Paul said,
"In Him dwelleth all the fulness of the Godhead bodily."
As Jesus was the manifestation of God where man could
see and comprehend Him, so spiritual power is often the
manifestation of Jesus where men can see and comprehend
Him by His effects in the actual world. Since He was
withdrawn from our sight at the Ascension, we must "see"
Him in His footprints, in His effects. We must see Him in
the manifestation of His power.

From the beginning, men have been drawn to Him by
His power. You can take it on the lowest level, where after
He came into the picture, the five thousand had enough to
eat, some of whom certainly believed in Him because they
saw the loaves and fishes, the modern counterpart of which
is that rather childish and definitely selfish view of Christianity which wants to use our faith in the Lord Jesus Christ
to get what we want.

Or you can take it on the highest level, where devout and

reasonable men and women were absolutely convinced that Jesus had risen from the dead and "become the first-fruits of them that slept." Both are manifestations of unusual, yes, of miraculous, and of divine power. With some restraint, Jesus was willing to call on all the power at His command to help men in their sickness and in their need.

The religion of Jesus, when it comes to us authentically, is always characterized by power. We see power in the very bad people made good. We see power as the moderately good and bad people come to realize that neither is good enough. We see power in the life held from an old defeat by a new charge of spiritual conviction. We see power when the sick are made well, not only by medicine, but by prayer, and any convinced Christian ought to be able to lead you into touch with persons in whose lives something like this has taken place.

We see power when the tensions which grip men's minds and bodies in this stressful time are released into quiet functioning and health. We see power when a light is lighted in a darkened mind that could not believe, but suddenly begins to believe because of the contagion of another's witness and faith.

The church is meant to be the channel and organ by which that spiritual power which is in Jesus is made available to man. Is your church like that? Are you yourself such a believer in power, such a receiver of power, such a channel of power, that it flows constantly into you and through you? If not, you ought to be, for it is part of your birthright as a Christian. Let us not beg off, and offer substitutes. The church is dropping down to a lower level and offering people "ersatz" and synthetic spiritual power—but nobody is fooled.

Power is *not just taking responsibility for the Church's work*. That is a very good thing, and we depend greatly on people who will do it. But it is not necessarily power. You can do a great stint of church work very much on your own steam, by self-effort, without any power needed from God and without any power being transmitted to other people.

Power is *not just efficiency*. It is a good thing to be as efficient as we can in Christ's work. But I can take you to churches that run with the utmost smoothness—the program is full and swift and runs like a clock—but it is all much more like a railroad station than it is like a real church of Christ. True power will usually manage to be efficient, but efficiency does not of itself constitute spiritual power.

Power is *not common sense*. The church is full of people with a lot of common sense. We abound in common sense. I would not say we always abound in spiritual power. The two are not in necessary conflict, and true spiritual power will be full of super common sense. But common sense by itself can cut the thread of spiritual power. I have seen it happen more times than one.

Power is *not intellectual smartness*. If it were, our modern universities and seminaries would be turning out better men than they did in the past, but it is doubtful if they are. A certain kind of spiritual power is very alert intellectually, and as smart as you can find men to be—witness the swift answers which Bryan Green gives his questioners concerning the intellectual matters of religion. Our Lord Himself was not above a witticism now and then. But one feels this came from power and did not constitute it.

Power is *not personal gifts and charm*. Those who have

them are blessed and, if they are rightly used, I think none of us will deny that they can be one channel of power. But they do not constitute power. How many men have I known, even in Christ's ministry, whose personal gifts and charm have led them astray from the Gospel, so they like to be set apart from the great body and common run of Christians, and to be something special and unique! This is not power—this is simple dramatics, and ought to be labelled so.

Power is *not points of view*. When our religion has been a long time with us, without the grace of renewal, when it has got stale and gone to seed, it continues on in viewpoints. It was born in power; it lives on in mere attitudes. A person is truly converted to Jesus Christ, and brought into the church; but time goes on, and this person becomes just an Evangelical or just an Anglo-Catholic, just a Liberal or just a Fundamentalist. The power is gone, but its corpse and echo remain in points of view. True evangelistic power is firsthand and original.

Many of us hold points of view within the faith, because they represent our intellectual convictions. But they are always dangerous, because pride, divisiveness, and even hostility often lie just beneath their surface. Seldom do they constitute power, and often they negate and under-cut it.

True spiritual power of the Christian order is a kind of possessedness. It arises in and flows through a life hid with Christ in God. Its source is the grace of our Lord Jesus Christ, and the potency of the Holy Spirit. True spiritual power is the child of two parents: the truth as it is re-vealed in Jesus and our own experience resulting upon our acceptance of Him and His truth. The objective factor is that the whole set of facts and truths, of historic events, and of interpretation of them, which is held by the church and set forth in the Bible. The subjective factor is what happens in the crucible of your life and mine when we accept that set of facts and truths and interpretations, and it begins to work in us. We have then a two-edged witness.

We witness to the truth as it is in Jesus, and we witness to the Christian experience as this transforms our own lives. If you take only the truth, and leave out the experience, you will probably become dogmatic and hard. If you take only the experience and leave out the truth, you will probably become woolly and amorphous and sentimental. But when you take both, and both are watered by the streams of grace, you have authentic spiritual power. Truth plus experience equals spiritual power—that is the formula.

Let me show you how spiritual power is manifested:

A YOUNG woman is deeply touched by a youth mission. She has had a steady upbringing in a formalistic church. She knows nothing of religion as power, but only as ceremony. She is not insincere; this is all she has known. But at the mission she sees that there is much more to Christianity than she has been accustomed to.

At first it baffles her, and she cannot understand it. Then follows a talk with someone who brings in the experience side as well as the truth side. This is a college girl with a keen mind. Suddenly the light begins to dawn—not only in her mind, but in her whole personality. Her face lights up and she says, "I begin to see!"

Much more was here than someone witnessing to her.

Here was the Spirit of truth guiding someone into the truth. It is a wonderful thing to see. Clear power has been poured forth.

A YOUNG man is stirred by the same mission. He makes an effort at surrendering himself to his Lord, but says it "didn't come off." Something else is needed—a talk with a sympathetic counselor. With enough time, the accumulated anxieties of a lifetime come to light—the unspoken horrors of the war, perhaps a slight, delayed reaction from it in wanting to be too much alone and aloof, a tangled human relationship, a wonder what the future should hold. And when these are sharpened a little, there comes a very simple prayer in which they are brought before God. And you see tense eyes grow quiet, and a tense frame relax, and there takes place what Agnes Sanford calls a healing of the memories. And he says, "I certainly do feel differently from the way I felt when I came in."

A WELL-EDUCATED, early-middle-aged man, happily married with children, is stricken with an illness. There is no religion in his home background. But in addition to what doctors and nurses can do, there is what some friends are doing, and that is praying. And in some way he is soon raised up, with scarcely a mark of illness upon him. And he comes to Christ's church and says, "I guess I am looking for somebody to thank." And there pours out another story of mounting spiritual hunger, arising very gradually and naturally and yet you cannot interpret it on quite a naturalistic plane.

Now he wants help in how to study the Bible. He wants to learn about the nature and meaning of the Church. He takes a long list of books to read. He wants to associate himself with Christ's people. He even considers putting his life to work in a place where he can exercise a greater Christian service. Allow for all the human factors in this, and yet here is a clear manifestation of spiritual power. Something of God has come into that man's life, and more will come.

A SMALL group of ministers meet. They are close friends in the Spirit, and have met before. Over a period of time, God has knit their hearts together in a fellowship that is not based on viewpoints, nor yet on personal congeniality, though they are congenial. And coming together again, they can open their hearts freely to one another.

They can talk about the work of the church, about its leadership, without constraint or self-seeking, because God has given them a selfless trust in each other. And inner feelings flow out in confidence, and what could not be said to many can be said to these. And here is simple, realistic, truthful, unselfish fellowship. It is something the world longs for, and often the church longs for, and does not find. The Spirit is there, and because the Spirit is there, power is there.

HERE are four places where authentic Christian spiritual power has come through. They are not majestic jets of power, like the Transfiguration, or the Resurrection, or Pentecost, but rather that same kind of power stepped down to mortal needs and capacities—so that you have a trans-figuration by the illumination of a girl's mind, so that you have a resurrection by awakening in the life of two men, so that you have a tiny echo of Pentecost, a little pint-size Pentecost, to fit the lives of modern ministers in New York. There is nothing here beyond us or outside our capacities, though for the time it may be these things are outside our experience.

My plea is for you to bring them inside your experience. It is so drab and dull when we do not know religion as power. We ourselves have such an inadequate taste of it that we hardly know what a good solid mouthful of it would be like. We give to the world such an inadequate picture of what Christianity is all about, for nothing is less attractive than the outwardness of religion without the inward power.

The church without power is a factory for hypocrites. But, worse than all, we must deeply disappoint and even offend God when we keep, as it were, a hand on the faucet, and tell Him we are not ready for the full flow of spiritual power, for we do not know where it would carry us, nor what it would do for us. There is scarcely a sin in all the calendar to compare with the shame of being willing in any way to hold back the amazing, beneficent, ever-willing power of God.

We are meant, every one of us, as Christ's children and servants and soldiers, to be both recipients of that power and transmitters of it. It is there for us, and there for those intended to receive it through us. Might we not all do very well to put aside everything else in this world but the search to know that power of God and pass it on to others?

Look back ten thousand years from now at the things that occupy our attention—the amusements, the garments, the emotional excitements, the search for money and worldly power and some thrill of the body—how shall they look then? And how shall the other look, our failure to search till we find the very power of God which comes to them who receive truly the Holy Spirit!

God bless us and make us discontent with standing anywhere but in the midst of the full flow of His grace and power, and with doing anything less than loosing that blessed power upon the sick and fearful and unreached and bewildered and seeking folk of our time, who will never in all their lives be satisfied till they find Christ, and through Him find the Holy Spirit, and through Him find the power which it is His alone to give. "Ye shall have power, after that the Holy Ghost is come upon you. . . ."

15.

Can Our Kind of Church Change Our Kind of World?

The Real Mission of the Church

THE CHURCH EXISTS to convey to all men the message of Christ and to build the kingdom of God in the earth. It has no reason for being apart from the fulfillment of this supreme and destined task.

The church is therefore not an end but a means. It was not the church which "God so loved that He gave His only begotten Son," but the world. The church is the company of those who, having heard the message of Christ, responded, discovered the meaning of life in Him, and henceforth has but one aim, to reach all men for Him. The "means of grace" with which the church is endowed are not satisfactions for the comfort of the 'ins,' so much as gifts for their equipment and empowering as they seek to reach the 'outs.' The early apostolic Christian did not think of the church as merely a place for the shepherding of believers. Of course we are intended to receive training, knowledge, forgiveness, fellowship, and inspiration in the church; but these are for our strengthening in the battle to win the world for Christ. Dr. Brunner says, "The church exists by mission as fire exists by burning."

Its success or failure, therefore, is not to be determined by the state of its buildings, or the size of its membership, but solely by what it is doing to reach the untouched.

To read many of the church's pronouncements, to listen to many clergy "talk a good fight," one would think the church's task was clear to all its members. But when you take an honest look it is apparent that, in most places, it is so bogged down in its means that it has forgotten its ends. George Santayana once said that "fanaticism is redoubling your efforts when you have forgotten your aim." If that is fanaticism, do not look for it only in wild and emotional sects: look for it in staid and respectable churches, where what once were means are today pursued as ends.

Bishop Emrich of Michigan says on this point, "Some women's groups meet in order to raise money to meet the budget in order that they might have a place to meet to raise money to meet the budget." Most of our church work is occupied with rescuing local parishes from going under, or keeping them up to their old standards of prestige, or making them a howling outward success. The maintenance of our local churches is obviously necessary, but when they become ends in themselves, they cease to be true churches. However authentic their ancestry, they certainly cannot call themselves "apostolic" churches.

Go in and listen. What kind of preaching do you hear?

Can Our Kind of Church Change Our World? [145]

Sometimes it is the Word of God, fresh from Scripture—living contact with the needs of contemporary men. But how often instead it deals with some small piece of the Christian message, peripheral, powerless, even trivial, far from the heart and center of the Gospel. Canon Bryan Green once said to me that he was appalled at how little of the Gospel you hear preached in this country. Rather, it's nice little talks about how God loves you and will help you, all which is true enough; but where is the cross and repentance; where is the blazing light of the risen Christ; where is the message of conversion, commitment, and new life?

One does not expect every local clergyman to be a Savonarola or a Wesley, nor every Sunday sermon to be an apocalypse, but surely these little church essays must give way to something more exacting, more exciting, more inspiring, something closer to experience! To be told to be a little kinder, or to say our prayers more often, is not a call to a changed life, centered in Christ, spending itself for the Kingdom!

Our terms of admittance to the church are unbelievably cheap. A few hours or weeks of theological and ecclesiastical instruction, and people are baptized or confirmed. These services contain words of utmost meaning filled with Gospel truth, but how many people have any real conception of what they say when they answer, "Do you promise to follow Jesus Christ as your Lord and Saviour?" by saying "I do"? Candidates are more often brought into touch with an historically well-authenticated, theologically sound, ethically wise, and organizationally well-run institution, than with a life-transforming Christ who leads them into the stream of the Holy Spirit. Do not their lives and works show it afterward?

CHRISTIANITY has truly been called a religion of ecstasy. You cannot live in the presence of a risen Lord, and of His fiery Holy Spirit, without a continuous, graceful excitement burning in your soul. William James said religion was either a dull habit or an acute fever. Yet how many of us could possibly be described as having "an acute fever"? Many of us feel a slight flicker of excitement when we read or hear something that agrees with what we already believe. Some clergy take fire when criticizing Billy Graham and their eyes shine. When shall we find that in the great warfare of light against darkness in our time we are going to need the support of allies who may not be exactly to our personal taste, and learn that it is going to take all Christians working and pulling together to make headway against the storm of anti-Christ?

This accumulated spiritual failure is doing something to our people. We have hosts of people, faithful in attendance and service, who are frankly far from the Spirit of Christ, because all they have heard are the words. They have not seen and been part of a changed, dissatisfied, repenting, growing fellowship. They just go to church, and do church work. You know them—a woman always there, tight as bees-wax with her money, another with a stinging tongue, a vestryman with a notorious temper, clergy who just never "hear" their people. We are losing some of our people who are most in earnest. I know one devoted woman who comes of a distinguished ancestry who goes to the Holy Communion at 8 o'clock in her own church, and at 11 o'clock goes elsewhere because she says she simply finds no spiritual help in her own church. The other church to which she goes is a place filled with the Holy Spirit and expectation and where things happen to people that release them into joyous Christian faith and witness. It is the church itself which has pushed her out.

Fine words, and uninspired directives from headquarters, based upon great aspirations but little concrete experience in the release of power in people and groups, is the blind leading the blind. When all else fails, there is always the blessed "commission" to "study" the subject. A layman told me he is on a diocesan commission that will come up, in three years, with the answer to what the church needs. I reminded him that our Lord did His whole public work in less time than that, created a team and fellowship but never a commission, and that we might just not have three years before the catastrophe falls which may reduce us to little else than a struggle for survival, if we have even that.

Let's face it—we create committees and commissions and take up the time of our best laymen with things that cannot possibly awaken the church or change the world, because we do not know what else to tell them to do. There simply is no great, inspired leadership that, beginning with repentance for our obvious and abject spiritual failures, prays to God for light, and leads, not by words but by the release of spiritual power. If the Holy Spirit is not dead, He can still speak. But what He says may cause us to go outside the ecclesiastical formulae, as it will most certainly guide us to do some things we have not been doing.

It must be perfectly obvious that the whole church, from top to bottom, needs a deeper conversion, a profounder experience of the power of the Holy Spirit. We have often recognized this, then gone about expecting it to happen through sterile and ineffectual means. Awakening in history has never come from ecclesiastics getting together to "do something." It has come from inspired nobodies, whom first the church ignored, then condemned, then (if they got powerful) took over, and finally domesticated. It is of no use to look for hope in time-consuming, money-spending commissions that wind up in long reports nobody reads. Let us look to see where the Holy Spirit is at work. Maybe we can learn something.

There are movements today where the Holy Spirit is at work. If we deny this, we sin against the Holy Spirit; for to deny His evident work in the hearts of men must be the supreme blasphemy. Moreover, the Holy Spirit is strangely democratic, and works where some people don't quite think He should. There are movements of the Holy Spirit in our time which could not possibly have been denominational in their origin or operation, yet are clearly arms of the church and work with the church just as far as the church will let them.

In addition to these, there are many local churches where you can find a steadily working evangelism going on all the time. The work being done in them is the kind that enables laymen to find a new life and then trains them to transmit it to others and to apply it in their own situations. Commissions for study by a lot of well-intentioned, inexperienced men are bound to come up with theoretical, untested ideas. You don't get a living baby by buying a pair of legs, a pair of arms, a torso and a head, and sewing them together. A baby is an organic product. Live things spring from live things, not inorganic pieces brought together.

Instances of just what the church needs are already at hand. They need not be sought, and they cannot be found, by theoretical explorations. No one has yet created plant or human life: you have to experiment with live things. It is so with the things of the Spirit. God has never left Himself without a witness, without some living break-throughs of His Holy Spirit. Why is the organized church so reluctant to look for its answer in out-of-the-way places, at the place where the Holy Spirit is working with un-ideal human beings and producing it? Are our specifications better than His? They are certainly different. The difficulty is, He seems to produce something even through His fallible means, while our beautiful theories are wonderfully sterile. Some stuffy leaders expect evangelism just to benefit their parishes. I think the Holy Spirit rejects outright such narrowness. I have never known Him to work in such limited ways.

God did not plant in the world the idea of rosebushes, or of human beings. He put plants and people into His creation. Men have done marvelous things with plant and animal experimentation. But nobody has created life. That seems still God's own prerogative. There are ways of awakening open to us. They are to be found and seen and examined and borrowed from and multiplied. They have happened through inspired, exploring, trial-and-error men and movements.

Two kinds of men stand between the church and learning from such men and movements.

There are the bureaucrats who see everything in terms of organizations and become dictators at heart for the thing "headquarters" has accepted and began to stand for.

These ecclesiastical "organization men" are frequently the enemies of spiritual awakening. It is to their personal interest, and it is part of their theoretical orientation, that the great organization is everything, the small organism of no importance. Subtly or openly, they fight true awakening. If there be a greater sin against the Holy Ghost than to try to stop His work, I do not know what it could be.

Then there are the local clergy and laymen, not the lazy and spiritually cold, but often the dedicated and spiritually warm men and women, who somehow long ago made up their minds just what they liked in the church and just how far they intended to go. They are good, kind, hard-working people—the "salt of the earth" kind of people. But they are deeply inured to doing it in a particular fashion. You cannot get them to ask themselves the question, Is all this getting anywhere? Will my kind of work multiplied lead to the awakening of the church, so that with dedication and passion it would get under its real task in the world and give everything it has to its accomplishment? I have seen such men brought face to face with opportunities to consider such awakening, look straight at them, and reject even the opportunity to investigate them! Why? They are living on ignorance or prejudice. Why the refusal even to investigate? I think the reason may be very simple. These other movements challenge and convict them of spiritual ineptitude and ineffectiveness. They know they would have to change their lives and their ways radically, and they draw back in craven fear. Dr. Alan Walker, reporting on the Graham meetings in Australia, said, "As people surged forward to register 'decisions for Christ' many a Christian minister recognized in his heart that he had been unfaithful, content merely to influence people rather than to seek a commitment of the will." Faced with such a challenge, you either try to meet it, or you turn away from it, determined to fight the thing which put it in front of your nose.

I have come to the sad and reluctant conclusion that the church is itself the great stumbling block. I do not mean the non-attenders and the pagan hangers-on. I mean the best clergy and laymen who are devoted, but devoted to the inadequate ways of organizational religion. These men and women are not only "conservative" about the faith, which is right; they are "conservative" about their own growth and willingness to change and learn, which is wrong. They will have their little church committees and commissions that have produced little or nothing in the past. They will keep up their own little faithful rites, giving their offerings, serving their little organizations, knowing all the time how futile the whole thing is when it comes to reaching the pagans in their own neighborhood, let alone those in the ends of the earth. Here is the blockage—not in the church's problem people, but in its good people who will not face their own great sin of spiritual ineffectiveness. It is a sin made greater because there are people in the world who can at least give them a lead about a much better way, a glimpse of what real awakening might be and would cost at the personal, parochial, Communion-wide level.

This universal awakening is the one thing that should concern us, and the one test of the consecration of our lives and the effectiveness. It is time to say it. It is not the strength of our enemies that holds us back. It is our own weakness. The church's best people who will learn no more and move no further, nor faster—are our stumbling block.

These people have the field. The world thinks this is all Christianity can do. Such folk usually dislike the word "witness," but they do it all the time, and the witness they give is a sad mockery of apostolic, Spirit-filled, life-transforming Christianity. The trouble lies, not with hard-to-convince intellectuals, nor indifferent young people, nor pagans that look the other way—the trouble lies with so-called Christians who hold convictions but are not living convincing lives, and with so many shopworn church folk with their dull, lustreless religion.

The world is living fast. Everywhere is great scientific achievement. There is fear in every sensitive heart. There is drivenness, want of satisfying emotion, increase of un-reason, rebellion, loss of regard for personality, easy dismissal of the spiritual as irrelevant or even non-existent. There is gnawing loneliness, and vague, intense bitterness, besides the eternal fact that "most men live lives of quiet desperation." Bishop Huddleston says, "The issue of our day is the issue of communicating to a pagan, post-Christian world: a world which has heard a language and relegated it to the four walls of a church; a world which will only hear the language again if it can come with a freshness, a stimulus, a shining sparkle." Are these three things characteristic of our church and our people—"freshness, stimulus, shining sparkle"? You and I know well that they are not. And that means that this kind of a church cannot change this kind of a world. It can hardly get into conversation with it.

WHAT, then, shall we do?

First, let us admit our almost wholesale failure, while giving thanks for what God has been able to do in spite of us. If we remain convinced that we are basically "all right," and just need a little polishing up, we shall not seek a remedy that goes deep enough to heal, nor find an answer sufficient to empower. Jim Rayburn, founder of Young Life says, "We started by knowing something was wrong." We have long known this. Let us admit it, confess it, repent of it.

Second, let us go on our knees in a deep and penitent surrender to God for our sins—not just other peoples'. The most we can give is ourselves. If this is to differ from what we have said and done before, we may need to seek out some kind of confessor and let some other human being know about what we are surrendering this time. It may take a conference, where there is great spiritual power let loose, for us to see in others what needs to happen in us. An outstanding clergyman said he learned more at a Faith at Work conference than he had in seminary and ten years of ministry. There is no substitute for organic fire moving through one and then another, as fire moves through contiguous coals. The church is full of people who have never seen it, who fear it, and who eschew it. They are always talking about "The Church," but a lot of them do not know what the Spirit-filled body really is.

Third, let us pray. We all know something of private prayer, and prayer in church. We must learn another kind —prayer with others, "where two or three are gathered together," as Jesus said. The shyness and self-consciousness that keep many from any kind of expression of their religion is their great sin. Prayer which desires, but does not expect, is debilitating. We need small groups of praying people all over—in the churches and outside them.

Fourth, we need the strengthening fellowship of such groups. We come to know and love these people, so that we can share together in honesty our victories and our defeats. Many people shrink from giving of themselves. They are about as mature emotionally as a child who fears to go into a room where there are other children. The reformation and renewal of the church begin with you. Increasingly there should be such friendliness, joy, and power released in these groups that others can be brought in to get some idea what Christian experience is, how to come into it, and how it enhances and transforms daily life.

Fifth, we shall then be able to witness to others, by life and by word. When the "shine" and "sparkle" are there, it will not be hard to open the conversation. It is not a matter of personality. It is a matter of grace. It will happen not only with individuals, but the Holy Spirit will begin changing homes, businesses, communities. The sharing of an experience in which we can all participate is more convincing than declaring a faith in which we believe. The church is going to have to justify its presence and make its faith known in this very practical world—not by theoretical arguments coming from scholars' studies, or pulpits, but by facing the concrete needs in the world, and showing that it has the real solution to them by solving them. Theoretical defense of the faith may touch the few. The many will only be touched by practical demonstrations of the workableness of the faith when really tried. There are hundreds of people whose lives are patent demonstrations of these things.

Am I asking the church to change completely the philosophy of its work? Yes, I am. I have no doubt about the

Credo

As I sit in the study on a beautiful, cool August afternoon, I look back with many thanks. It has been a great run. I wouldn't have missed it for anything. Much could and should have been better, and I have, by no means, done what I should have done with all that I have been given. But the over-all experience of being alive has been a thrilling experience. I believe that death is a doorway to more of it; clearer, cleaner, better, with more of the secret opened than locked. I do not feel much confidence in myself as regards all this, for very few have ever "deserved" eternal life. But with Christ's atonement and Him gone on before, I have neither doubt nor fear whether I am left here a brief time or long one. I believe that I shall see Him and know Him, and that eternity will be an endless opportunity to consort with the great souls and the lesser ones who have entered into the freedom of the heavenly city. It is His forgiveness and grace that give confidence and not merits of our own. But again I say, it's been a great run. I'm thankful for it and for all the people who have helped to make it so, and especially those closest and dearest to me.

—SAMUEL MOOR SHOEMAKER

So I Stay Near the Door

An Apologia for My Life

I stay near the door.
I neither go too far in, nor stay too far out,
The door is the most important door in the world—
It is the door through which men walk when they find God.
There's no use my going way inside, and staying there,
When so many are still outside and they, as much as I,
Crave to know where the door is.
And all that so many ever find
Is only the wall where a door ought to be.
They creep along the wall like blind men,
With outstretched, groping hands,
Feeling for a door, knowing there must be a door,
Yet they never find it . . .
So I stay near the door.

The most tremendous thing in the world
Is for men to find that door—the door to God.
The most important thing any man can do
Is to take hold of one of those blind, groping hands,
And put it on the latch—the latch that only clicks
And opens to the man's own touch.
Men die outside that door, as starving beggars die
On cold nights in cruel cities in the dead of winter—

Die for want of what is within their grasp.
They live, on the other side of it—live because they have
        found it.
Nothing else matters compared to helping them find it,
And open it, and walk in, and find Him . . .
So I stay near the door.

Go in, great saints, go all the way in—
Go way down into the cavernous cellars,
And way up into the spacious attics—
It is a vast, roomy house, this house where God is.
Go into the deepest of hidden casements,
Of withdrawal, of silence, of sainthood.
Some must inhabit those inner rooms,
And know the depths and heights of God,
And call outside to the rest of us how wonderful it is.
Sometimes I take a deeper look in,
Sometimes venture in a little farther;
But my place seems closer to the opening . . .
So I stay near the door.

There is another reason why I stay there.
Some people get part way in and become afraid
Lest God and the zeal of His house devour them;
For God is so very great, and asks all of us.
And these people feel a cosmic claustrophobia,
And want to get out. "Let me out!" they cry.
And the people way inside only terrify them more.
Somebody must be by the door to tell them that they are
        spoiled
For the old life, they have seen too much:
Once taste God, and nothing but God will do any more.
Somebody must be watching for the frightened
Who seek to sneak out just where they came in,
To tell them how much better it is inside.

So I Stay Near the Door [159]

The people too far in do not see how near these are
To leaving—preoccupied with the wonder of it all.
Somebody must watch for those who have entered the door,
But would like to run away. So for them, too,
I stay near the door.
I admire the people who go way in.
But I wish they would not forget how it was
Before they got in. Then they would be able to help
The people who have not yet even found the door,
Or the people who want to run away again from God.
You can go in too deeply, and stay in too long,
And forget the people outside the door.
As for me, I shall take my old accustomed place,
Near enough to God to hear Him, and know He is there,
But not so far from men as not to hear them,
And remember they are there, too.
Where? Outside the door—
Thousands of them, millions of them.
But—more important for me—
One of them, two of them, ten of them,
Whose hands I am intended to put on the latch.
So I shall stay by the door and wait
For those who seek it.
"I had rather be a door-keeper . . ."
So I stay near the door.